LOST WORKS

❧ LOST WORKS ❧

Daniel Roberts

iUniverse, Inc.
New York   Bloomington

Lost Works

iUniverse books may be ordered through booksellers or by contacting:

iUniverse
1663 Liberty Drive
Bloomington, IN 47403
www.iuniverse.com
1-800-Authors (1-800-288-4677)

Because of the dynamic nature of the Internet, any Web addresses or links contained in this book may have changed since publication and may no longer be valid. The views expressed in this work are solely those of the author and do not necessarily reflect the views of the publisher, and the publisher hereby disclaims any responsibility for them.

ISBN: 978-1-4502-6115-9 (sc)
ISBN: 978-1-4502-6117-3 (dj)
ISBN: 978-1-4502-6116-6 (ebk)

Library of Congress Control Number: 2010914132

Printed in the United States of America

iUniverse rev. date: 09/16/2010

Acknowledgments

For my family, friends, inspirations. For the world of many hearts and minds, many religions and people, but of one race and one faith, humanity.

Of light and shadow and the Order of Love and Knowledge

A masterpiece cannot be created without light and shadow. Light is the focal point of self knowledge around which we paint our lives upon the canvas of life. Our good intentions paint a brilliancy of color that make the colors of this world be a dim reflection of our perception of such hues and tone. From our intentions we paint our actions upon the canvas of life we express our love, trust, faithful, loyal, bravery, talents, our good will, what we desire to experience, and how we may help, heal, inspire or entertain through expressing our abilities around the focal point of our self knowledge. The shadow exists as a remembrance of the mistakes we have made that is cast from the color that we have painted through our intentions but formed from our inability to cope with certain situations that had merited our virtue while expressing our desires or ego moved by our will. These shadows are seen from self reflection as the focal point of our self knowledge gives us depth on the life as we move into the light as we grow and deepen our perception. We sometimes do not see the shadow of our mistakes because we fail to understand our self enough to care enough to recognize what we did wrong but will gladly hold others to their mistakes. We are more focused on other peoples mistakes which, have us feel we are impervious to making mistakes despite having made them in our life because we lack the depth perception on our life from the light of our self knowledge being to dim to define the colors that have cast but meager shadows upon our canvas. The focal point of light displays shadows within this canvas of our life as they are brought out by our self knowledge as the shadows exist as being an afterthought of what we should and could have done so we may extend the light of self knowledge to create a more colorful life with less shadow as we paint our intentions in the light of knowledge but with a heart to know. Meaning, through the depth of self knowledge the light that exist as a focal point we paint more of our passions around as we seek to achieve in life by understanding our self and the nature of self and humanity. Even though the should haves and could haves don't exist only the do's and don'ts we always have regrets of a time we wished we could have done differently. Our lack of knowledge of being in the situations that merit our virtue gets in the way of doing what is right from our lack of experience or from our desires hindering our judgment to do what is right. Hindsight is always twenty-twenty but from our lack of experience do we make mistakes but is recognized as being such from the self knowledge we have gained from our open conscious which, defines life with a stronger clarity and sharpness as we gain discernment, as we know the proper way to behave in the situations that evoke emotion which is a life long growing process. It is as if clarity increases as the focal point of self knowledge gives us depth on life in the light of how to treat each other but also gives us a depth on life to bring clarity into necessity and what isn't a necessity as if we sort the shaft from the wheat to refine our behavior around how to gain through our abilities but without contention. Nature's way having us gain but avoid suffering through our behavior rises through the Mind as our self knowledge has our abilities be refined so that actions will pose no contention despite competing with self to gain so that suffering will no longer be in Mind but be avoided through a conscious effort. Life becomes more colorful.

By letting God into our life it does not mean he takes control of our life but he steers our life through us from our willingness to live better by understanding the nature of his will and how that is one with survival which is through virtue which leads to an Order of Love and

Knowledge to bring forth peace through words and action and stability through virtue to have us rely upon acting without contention and not surviving through hate or violence but rather through virtue. Nature naturally made us virtuous to not only survive but to live. Virtue was Nature's way to have us live as we avoid suffering to keep the body alive as we evolved. Virtue established from our senses despite being from a body and Mind connection. In heaven we are naturally virtuous from having a body and being aware of the body like in life but in heaven they would have an enlightened conscious to have virtue move unimpeded as it comes from the mind. Our very self is virtuous and from there do we feel dishonored or disrespected because the values that virtues posses reflects worth because value is worth which would therefore show Self worth through virtue to have virtue be an eternal value of self worth that is equal for all human beings from all human beings being naturally virtuous. Virtue is the nature of our center from where we find the love of virtue from training to reinforce and build self worth but also from a deepening of the conscious as we find the value of our virtue so that we may obtain what we love but in a manner where we secure self. And it is knowledge that is part of a dependant system that has the eternality of all meanings that exist static be in there individuality so meaning can be re-gathered through the conscious to say meaning is an eternal static constant, for water has always been wet and fluid before I was born to have me in my temporality bring recognition to an eternal meaning so that in my ignorance I may say I have gained knowledge so that the conscious which is actualized from being a potential of creation may connect with knowledge in a dependant system to have the conscious be a part of the knowledge gained from a dependant system to say there is a gathering of knowledge from eternal meanings. It is only connecting the feelings of virtue to functions so that we may reinforce virtuous behavior to deepen consciousness and being conscientious around given tasks so that value can be present and be shown so that familiarity will train virtuous behavior from feeling the good received from virtue which touches on their self worth(virtuous self) to be positively reinforced from uniting self worth to given tasks(functions) so that values(principles) will be obtained to keep self worth motivated and the conscious secure which in turn effects the ego from attachment to reinforce both a love of virtue as they learn to gain, give, and avoid suffering from a conscious effort but also has our attachment of worth effect our ego as we obtain a specialness of self, a confidence which is healthy but not when one's excessive pride makes him miscalculate his own actions or others or compete in an egotistical manner from obtaining dependancy on looks and a certain behavior that has one gain and obtain self worth as one competes. So every time we feel upset or our ego is hurt it is from our innate and eternal virtuous self being put at risk through humans competing, gaining to have us feel a violation of virtue was present, or we didn't try hard enough which means we could have been more responsible, honest, etc., and is actualized through the conscious but with an awareness of the body so that we may know what we feel, to feel what we know, as we connect the heart an mind so that principles can be established from bringing Order around securing the conscious through the feeling of virtue moved by love to build self worth to keep the virtuous self secure and centered as one gains. This way we find value in life from the connection we make through our emotional self so that attachments can be made to benefit the psyche like within a relationship, to form principles around sustaining self worth between them through love motivating the value of their virtuous self to treat that person right(value), so by treating them as a reflection of self, one feel's self worth, as we show appreciation for what we value. The ego then becomes effected through attachment to influence self esteem so that in a relationship behavior will be adopted around stabilizing self esteem for both people so that there virtuous self may branch towards obtaining principles(rules/values) around what they desire about each other and to keep that alive. Even though the seven deadly sins are Vices, untrustworthiness, irresponsibility, unfaithfulness, etc., occurs when one's vice is lust, vanity, sloth, etc., which makes the complementary opposite of virtue be Vice but experienced through desires to gain to violate other's virtues to obtain gratification for self or expressed out of ignorance from needing to find the value of virtue so that one will grow to be more honest, trustworthy, etc., as they get older. Ignorance from the growing process, addictions, and attachments, have us be Vice oriented from how we obtain feelings of self worth from our behavior and stabilizing the conscious as we gain and avoid suffering. Vice is more recognizably known for being body oriented as our desires move our will but is also psychological due to how behavior supports the ego and feelings of self worth around valuing what we desire so that as we may approach being unfaithful or disrespectful it is to gain satisfaction for the body or secure position to feel respected but ultimately such desires is to supplement their psychological well being as they build around stabilizing what they can gain. Both vice and virtue are supported by how it secures the ego as we learn to gain and avoid suffering to keep the virtuous self stable so that we may still feel dishonored or disrespected despite disrespecting others. It may be hypocritical but is part of the growing process.

The Order of Love and Knowledge has virtue be the center as we stay open to knowledge from our love. This is Order rising itself through Chaos, a system with uncertainty. As the creation of life met the adversity and unpredictability that Chaos brings within the physical plane to evolve the body and it's behavior around sustaining the bodies homeostasis and nurture symmetry in an asymmetrical plane as pressure nurtured joints and the elongation of the digits to have us cope with the force from changing the inertial course as we moved and applied pressure to nurture symmetry from adversity. Two eyes, two ears, nostrils, formed symmetrically as sensitivity forced change to have adversity effect how we formed symmetrically but how it is done genetically is a mystery to me. And as intellectual capacities grew, we grew into the recognition of the mechanics and motion of the nature of life to explain the dimension of our environment as we included time with distance to plan and think dimensionally. Patterns and symmetries formed in a dependant system of asymmetry caused by the Order of growth being from an energy dependant system that is forced into a volumetric dependancy from volume being generated for mass as it poses an inequality relative to the vacuum to generate a force of gravity to ensure statics so that symmetry will rise through the Order of dependancy and growth but will face the adversity of force that creates asymmetry. As we grew intellectually, our ability to communicate increased to have security and insecurity created from competing amongst a fertile Planet that created Dinosaur and fish to the evolving mammals, as we were preyed upon and delt with poisonous plants and insects to instill feelings of being territorial to gain security amongst our environment due to the fight or flight response existing so that through being territorial we kept ourselves stable and even gained security through our ego to compete and obtain security as we competed for dominance which creates feelings of security through harm or hate as we measured life out of fear to gain security or dominance more strongly which had harm and hate rise upward as our conscious deepened as we evolved through the adversity that Chaos brings from being part of the dependancy of knowledge so that as we understood the nature of our environment we lived with meaning but in the light of peace. We went from being a peaceful species into being a territorial species that became smarter in how they took and competed amongst each other to create feelings of hate and harm from taking from each other physically and emotionally. It is as if consciousness evolved as it was pulled from within the evolution of life from the stimulosus put upon the organism/species causing primary movement from the evolving faculties of the organism be stimulated by the senses to have us move based on thermal energy and toward food sources to then have us fight or flee based on experiencing pain and loss repeatedly over hundreds of thousands of years to give us the faculty of fighting or fleeing as we relied highly upon sight and sound from being sense oriented and not dimensional thinkers. We evolved from the cellular mass being stimulated to move without thinking to have the senses like the eyes, ears, and nose stimulate the limbic system to move our animal self to have consciousness be not as deep from the brain not being as evolved to allow stronger self awareness despite being self aware through the will of the form but would be influenced highly upon the senses. At this point we know the nature of our food source and it's behavior to have us judge but did not rise to the point of being planners despite starting to judge distance, behavior, and time to have us start planning. The formation of the senses brought dimension to our environment so that as we evolved, we evolved to understand the nature of our environment in greater depth and understand each other. Listening skills and speaking gave way to evolve communication as our hearing and speech faculty within the brain strengthened which had us evolve our intellectual capacity and be dimensional thinkers through listening and speaking which had us understand the nature of our environment with greater depth and started planning as we evolved which gave way to a more peaceful way through having more control which was balanced by mans desires and lack of control as the brain and consciousness gave us more control through planning a peaceful/secure way. We started planning early on as we gained a depth of understanding on the nature of our environment and even from the behavior of food sources that stimulated our senses through sight and scent to have us start planning through understanding the nature of food sources. The genetic code seemed to have been created from a metabolic dependancy to decrease decay rate from the kinetics of catalysis creating a metabolic rate that kept the code alive(moving forward in time)? How amino acids varied themselves relative to the sugar helix is unknown to me but since Order arranges itself through dependancy the code would have been dependant upon itself and formed logical sequences through the dependancy. Cellular respiration became more efficient relative to the density of oxygen extracted from the atmosphere from the development of the lungs nurturing a four chambered heart as the lungs evolved to better handle the atmospheric condition early in evolutionary history when we were within the water. Does this mean we at first extracted oxygen from the water to then obtain a respiratory system that extracted oxygen from the air? To know that we evolved from the water and oxygen is necessary for metabolism is to know that we extracted oxygen from a water source before we evolved lungs and a four chambered heart while within the water.

As life adds force within the Universe from being a chemical mass replicating itself over time, it adds to the field of gravity within the vacuum, not from a displacement of mass alone but from a synthesis of a denser mass. Like stars created from a strong energy density of oppositely charged particles uniting to create atoms from the time of the Big Bang to create stars that form denser elements like carbon and iron that increases force within the Universe as the Universe expands to regain it's initial gravity value it had when it was a singularity, the time for the creation of life is increasing force within the Universe from chemical synthesis. Not from adding protons or electrons to the Universe but increasing density of mass and replicating that mass(life) to increase force within the Universe. Such mass has the ability of self reflection, can think backwards and forwards in time to have our consciousness be a time period of Life that is a measure in time from needing the proper incubation conditions to create it. Understanding Order would derive from growth from mass being formed from displacement but also adding mass to the Earth and adding force within the Universe over time so that we may understand the Order of knowledge from pattern learning emerging through the evolution of the body from repetitive cycling from the senses nurturing identification relative to the senses so that when a pattern is recognized a dimensional understanding is garnered and the environment will trigger releases to form instincts relative to security over hundreds of millions of years of evolution. The pattern of adversity or to obtain nourishment formed our instincts and increased memory as a response to the patterns learned in stimulating our mass from the food source to have us remember our food source as well as memory increased to keep the body from enacting in stress to secure and stabilize the metabolic rate from the evolving memory keeping the life form secure to keep the fight an flight response from happening more often. A Universe of complementary opposites formed a complementary opposite way of thinking as such a way was developed from feeling hot and cold, recognizing light and dark, hungry and full, to have patterns emerge from our awareness drawing dimension to a dependant system to find the dependancy knowledge has despite the eternal meanings held static as the conscious becomes part of a working dependant Order of knowledge so that as knowledge is gained from our awareness it will have us naturally move towards order and peace as we find a pattern of least resistance as we grow. This has us find strength of mind and body to live in a manner where we find less resistance to obtain what we want despite behavior being bad or good. Since statics can be actualized through the Mind than the Mind is aware of an unchanging principle or rule despite the dependancy of knowledge so that from the statics of meaning a harmony is generated through dependancy to create knowing and therefore awareness from being part of the dependancy of knowledge so that we may obtain perception through our understanding despite such knowledge being eternally static to have the Mind be a part of a static awareness as if the conscious remains static as it is eternal despite it being a dependant function. Even though knowledge is meaning, knowledge is acquisition, a garnering through dependancy to have us recognize the eternality and statics of meanings from and within our temporality. A static consciousness would be one with the statics of meanings but together through a dependancy they generate cognition as our awareness is actualized within a dependant system of the physical plane generating motion to unite God despite the statics of the conscious. It would be like the Mind recognizing the body as cognition is generated through our awareness to then have us say virtue is what it is from it being part of the essence of our soul's awareness. Even though every person has a soul it is not the physical world that creates the soul despite nature giving it, a physical conception and the being of virtue. That would create a filling of God. Reincarnation and Preordination allows a soul for every person as if the soul is part of conservation relative to the existence of time(physical plane) so that if five people are alive there would be five souls but if two people die the three souls would exist living as the other two go to God so that God would remain a quantity that is a constant that is a sticky potential that unites with the physical plane as life is generated over time. Like two cogs moving each other, the cycle of reincarnation meets the life cycle of generation and decay within the physical plane as if they work under a principle of conservation in time as God is forced into creation by the generation of life to move the cog(God). If the physical plane created souls through genetic inheritance then that would be a filling of God and therefore God would be incomplete, empty, imperfect from filling God with energy. The physical plane has an inequality generating motion and God enacts in closing the inequality to be a part of the system. A system of constant change and dependancy. Since God is eternal he fills life through the soul and his energy for plants. Not life filling God. Life would only stimulate God to enact in God knowing from his eternal meanings being activated through cognition so that God may know in time despite understanding eternally. Life would only stimulate God to have his souls enact in knowing as part of the dependant system of knowing so that as we learn does God learn through our individuality. Despite God having a static conscious the dependancy life has on God to conserve it's potential has his conscious be stimulated so that acquisition for God can be obtained in time as cognition stimulates statics in a harmony to generate knowing in time for God. The filling of God from the connection between life and him to represent transference of energy as "cogs" move, would have life create an imprint in time, not necessarily a filling of God with information but rather

Ordered arrangements of knowledge out of the statics of meanings so that we may have information from God being part of the dependancy of time but has God remain conserved despite the uncertainty from a force inequality within the physical plane having the wind not blow a leaf in the same position twice which is like saying knowledge is a moving forward in time which has each experience be new, as new experiences occur to give God knowing as meaning arranges itself to give us information over time. God would be growing into himself as souls live and transfer information to God so that a soul that returns to God would not fill God with information. The souls would be growing through purpose which is like saying God already understands we just have to grow into that understanding which would mean God would be filling himself from being one with time despite God remaining static so that eternal understanding can be seen as a growing into oneself as God remains conserved. So, that which is gained as information as time passes will not stick with God for an eternity as life ceases to exist. All that can and will be created is held in an eternal understanding from the nature of the conscious being a part of the dependancy of knowledge so that the soul will give meaning to knowledge not knowledge giving meaning to the soul as all that can and will be created through knowing already existing despite it being placed in different Orders from being within the dimension of time. When life pulls God back into creation the statics of meanings will remain, so that a new imprintation will occur to give us information once more but arranged differently. The transference of energy from God to the life cog would be the force of will to generate the movement of the cog(life) despite God being deep within nature due to our understanding of cells and genetics was already understood by God so that we may know in our temporality which means, God is deep within nature to have eternal meanings like the soul exist to connect with an infinite knowing to be a part of time. Nature is like a root that remains constant so that knowledge may follow guidelines for cognition as the conscious remains static despite imprinting nature as a guideline to the conscious to have God recognize the nature of his awareness as the Mind and Body unite. When the life cog is not there God exists as a conserved potential waiting for the life cog to spin to bring God into time and what would be a gathering of knowledge despite knowledge already being filled with meaning so an arrangement of knowledge can be created over time. The nature of the constantly changing empirical world has nature be the basic guideline from where knowledge can be constantly produced and placed in different orders as time passes. For instance, we have free will which allows us to make choices to have God obtain unique pieces of knowledge despite meaning being static to have understanding be eternal as knowledge arranges itself in a dependant system so that information will be created as time moves forward despite it being only an imprint of understanding due to the existence of the eternal meanings and the eternal and static conscious enacting in the cycle of dependancy and conservation.

Gravity, thermal energy, hydrostatic pressure and distilled chemicals within a aqueous solution had all animals evolve from the water. The sensitivity of the eye and its ability to handle the amounts of radiation it does to have us see would have our evolving species live within the water to have the water hinder radiation damage and as we obtained mobile capability we moved above the surface of the water where radiation was stronger, to have our eye evolve to handle the strength of light so that as we slowly left the water did our eyes confront the adversity of stronger radiation to build more rods and cones regulated by a stronger iris over billions of years of evolution. Sensitivity forces change and a strengthening, enlargement, and creation of organs even the appendix for processing food or extracting toxins from a hard to ingest or semi-toxic diet. Sensitivity forces changes that are evolutionary but also behaviorally to find coping mechanisms to deal with it's environment.

Sensitivity forces change, which happens in life as we adopt behavior that secures our psychological and emotional well being so that from it's familiarity it will give us security from being less sensitive. Sensitivity forcing change can have us pick up bad behavior to complement the way of our environment to avoid feelings of insecurity as we adopt behavior as a counter measure against feeling insecure as we fit the social norm. An insecurity that can be created from talking trash or getting into fights just to reinforce that behavior as we live with it's familiarity due to familiarity leading to conformity to breed a normalcy of contempt but is felt as being a social norm, to have us talk trash or get into fights more often as we extend hurting or taking away from others by controlling how people view us which is like controlling each others identities to make it harder on each other as we grow. We adopt behavior that will secure our psychological and emotional well being so that we can be free to live in peace amongst a competitive system. In our time period we extended talking trash and get into fights as we adopted behavior that secured our well being as a counter measure against it as we are made fun of or being dishonored or disrespected but familiarity through the growing process led to a normalcy of behavior and therefore it's acceptance. When our self is put at risk we feel it through how our virtues are being violated to have us feel dishonored, disrespected, trust being violated, nervous, anxious, angered, and through communication did we anger each other and start fights to have what was once not tolerated to be depicted for entertainment. We adopted the behavior we don't like happening to us and extended it outward as a countermeasure against the violence or trash talk just to secure our place amongst each other. It is natural for humans to judge and to talk about each other but to extend harmful words leads to depression or even violence. If familiarity has peer approval be based on violence or harmful words than that reinforces that behavior as familiarity breeds contempt to allow insensitivity as hardness breeds hardness. Sensitivity forces change which is natural but it is when we grow into insensitivity do we limit growth as we gain despite having the negative personal experiences be relied upon in memory to have us avoid suffering through a more conscientious way as we use empathy. We grow through trail and error despite it all. The sensitivity of evolution meets the sensitivity for the growing body and the deepening of the conscious as a human being grows. Just like giving a plant only so much light, not burn it. Sensitivity is part of the growing process and adversity is felt as we grow which makes us feel uncomfortable. To make each other more uncomfortable by extending negative comments outward had us adopt that behavior as a social norm to keep our ego secure amongst a population of many. We disrespected and dishonored each other. There was ten years of extreme violence, death, brining weapons to school, and mass murders. Just like you have a WWII generation and the values of society and how they desensitized themselves through communication, we have the Hippy time period that pushed our freedom of speech and press which deregulated what we can say and do about each other. Then you have the death in school time period and singling each other out, talking trash, or emasculating each other depicted in front of the world in the 80's and early 90's through the communication age which had us single each other out, provoke, and demean each other which was controlling there identity and how people viewed them on a worldly scale but familiarity of such behavior existed within our society and was shown to the world which reinforced the normalcy of trash talking that can lead to group hate as society slowly declined in the 90's despite the peace and money we had as a country. Since we publically emasculated, provoked, and demeaned males over the air waves it taught that we have a right to behave that way which led to provoking and demeaning women and children because how we treat males is how women treat women and children treat children. We taught that we have a right to judge, shame, control each others identities, etc.. Whenever humanity approaches a frontier like the wild west or with nuclear weapons our human nature will have fear or violence have us build to bring order. The communication age was a frontier and we pushed our rights to the point where it seemed as if they were violating each other's rights by saying you shouldn't have done what you did or this wouldn't have happened as if it was a way of governing by teaching repercussions but grew into a demeaning way as television shows went from group help and teaching in front of the world to talking trash to the person on stage to be entertained by seeing people demeaned. It was as if television was showing what would be in store for our generation as television depicted the behavior and reinforced the rights we practice as a society. The death and violence in schools is a time period which effected a time period of human growth for those in the free world and how we desensitize and popularize behavior for our children that has us gain but avoid suffering as familiarity bred contempt even through the camaraderie felt through group hate or shaming someone will be passed down as part of our basic nature to compete and have fun but also as a way of governing and getting someone to behave. Population growth and the money made from our freedoms naturally desensitized us but there was an alternating influence between convenience allowing us to have what we want as we grew from the 50's into the twenty first century to have divorce rates increase, mobility and the convince of being around the opposite sex more often lead to cheating, to being able to express our rights in the manner in which we sought fit, to then influence society on a grander scale through communications instead of having necessity influence values to have us talk less trash, get into less fights, and have serious relationships. Convenience influenced what we could do with our rights so that economically we profited from our human nature expressing itself which reinforces behavior through our rights as we grew amongst a population of many keeping themselves secure amongst a familiar behavior that secures one's self worth.

Sensitivity will be overcame by insensitivity in behavior to secure the animal self to secure the conscious as we unconsciously compete to gain and avoid suffering and secure our psychological and emotional well being as we behave through harmful ways, as virtue has to be reinforced due to virtues being feelings that is part of their nature that furthers growth and stability so that one may consciously compete to gain and avoid suffering through a more stable way. Striking at the ego is striking at the conscious and since the conscious evolves itself through virtue where sensitivity brings growth, competing through the ego changes the development for conscientious behavior. Striking at our ego is too much light and that will burn the plant and to have it compensate for the lack of growth will that person become too hard to cope with the hardness of it's environment or become too sensitive. We should grow to allow sensitivity so that conscientious behavior will be given through honor and respect so that as we grow we will not become too sensitive to life to have everything hurt us but just sensitive enough to allow the growth of thinking dimensionally and have a depth of understanding the conscious brings, as we live and experience life. Sensitivity forces change as much as insensitivity but to be insensitive forces one through more hardship as sensitivity allows exploration of the conscious and dimension or understand the nature of conscious through the ego using virtue and vice which are feelings, as insensitivity leads to a more destructive life style. Sensitivity must be allowed to allow progression and conscientious behavior. Insensitivity popularized becomes familiar through what is gained from what is at risk as we control how people view each other socially. It would be seen as a brave form of fun upheld by our constitutional right but practiced normally by our competitive nature. To gain and avoid suffering.

The sensitivity of the eye being born in an aqueous solution and constructed itself in the hydrostatics of water to hinder the damage to it's evolving eye and it's mass from handling the force from offsetting inertia from the mobility of our mass moving within the water to have us feel a force from momentum but also had the water lower the intensity in radiation, had the evolving cellular organism that evolved into an organism with a body, follow the food sources out of the water as early awareness was based on motor functions following recognition of food from it's senses even it's eyes which would have us be strongly attracted to the color and behavior of our food sources that would entice us into another atmospheric condition. From a hydrostatic depth and out where the force of gravity and the offsetting of inertia from motion creates a stronger force to have the fragility of our evolving mass deal with it's force to strengthen the body and balance for the brain, to strengthen the evolution of the life form. We followed the food source be if it was living food or plants out of the water. Our eye strengthened itself as it evolved to cope with the increase in radiation as we left the water to also strengthen and evolve the brain to recognize color at the same time balance was evolving for the brain from being in another atmospheric condition and following or finding the food source. This would force the brain to grow as if it were picking up on senses and balance and uniting them into a dimensional understanding with a dimensional imbalance from the ear or nose not being as strong but sight being stronger for instances which would force the brain to grow as senses attune themself from hearing in another atmospheric density where amplitude is higher and where scent travels faster as they evolve to bring a stronger clarity and depth into the nature of life and self relative to it's environment which would have lung capacity effect the sensitivity and evolution of scent cells from being within another atmospheric condition and having to take shorter breaths to move to evolve us from taking shorter breaths to smell to find the direction of scent in closer locations so that as our lung capacity grew we were able to stimulate the scent senses longer with time from longer inhales to find the direction of food which would have slowly nurtured the size of the scent organ as we traced scent for longer distances. Our scent faculty evolved relative to taste to have cooking food smell good but rotting flesh smell bad despite the vultures loving it which had taste evolve the scent senses so that repetitive occurrence of taste and scent create a similar diet for the species to have them obtain a fixed behavior to find the same or a similar sustenance of food from the remembrance of taste and pass it down genetically but in a manner where teaching occurred to effect large families within groups like birds or human families to ingrain instincts from being reared over hundreds of millions of years into behavior on how to follow the senses to obtain the same sustenance and escape harm so that by learning throughout evolution of following families they learned to react when each other reacts to learn what to do when the fight or flight response hits but also avoid the response and the increase in metabolic rate by reading the signs through it's intelligence but also ingrained taste and texture into a genetic palatability but relatively based on specie. Balance applied force on our ligaments and bone structure to have us fight against offsetting an inertial course to feel force as we grasped objects and walked upright. This allowed us to not be in survival mode all the time but allowed us to slow down and think from visually, hearing, and smelling the dimension of our environment to have familiarity create comfort at the expense of being territorial out of fear of losing security from being preyed upon by animals or away from the food source. Slowing down and thinking as well as communicating advanced our self awareness through deepening the conscious through deductive reasoning from the patterns observed and understood from communication as well as thinking about the nature of our environment despite it taking the right genetics to evolve the brain from basic stimulosus to a cognitive form. Basic stimulosus made us cognitive by avoiding suffering and obtaining sustenance which means cognition derived from our senses as thought slowly emerged based on our self awareness relative to our environment that we are putting sensual data to form dimension around our self. Just like in life, all that we feel, see, smell, taste, and touch is bringing dimension to your life relative to self to have you make decisions even around the ego through attachment.

Even though the ego is part of our consciousness and we can measure the values of virtue and vice through our ego as we feel the good that we create from how we secure our ego through virtue at the same time understand others and our own behavior as we feel and see the harm created from being untrustworthy or having our trust be violated amongst other virtues, the ego was created as a means for us to connect with each other not divide each other. The ego is effected by attachment to how we dress, how we talk, how we walk, how we look, but extends towards what we like, to bring identification to life through our emotional selves and it is that to which we have to secure, as our attachments effect our conscious and in life do we defend the ego to defend the conscious based on how our virtuous self is violated relative to that which the ego wants to defend but also by being made fun of does the insecurity from virtue being violated have us be more defensive as other ego's are built at the expense of others from them defending their attachments on life from defending the security of the ego and it's behavior expressed amongst a competitive system. So, no matter who it is, our feelings can be hurt to effect the ego but it is how strongly we attach our selves to how we walk, look, or talk which when made fun of do we obtain a sensitivity to effect our ego by it telling us that something is wrong with us as if it is a psychological way to separate people from a group as if our nature competes in this manner to have the most. Our virtuous selves have a more stable ego, for it identifies with the need behind life and the attachment through need but with the heart to release. The emotional standpoint of our ego is like a thermometer which can tell us that we can be burnt by both hot and cold. Our virtuous self(ego) knows that we don't like to be made fun all the time so that when we are made fun or bullied there is a violation of virtue such as respect, to have us get to the point of burning, which has us move away from our center where all is temperate. Meaning, the Mean point is contentment, the stability of our virtuous self, as we learn to live amongst each other to keep the virtuous self stable and continue to bring value into our lives. Values are one with virtue from what is gained from them so that we may say there is value and therefore strength of principle behind certain actions as virtue extends from self into the motion of life.

Despite how big a planet is life will be created within the hydrostatics of water and emerge. The larger the planet the stronger the gravity but water's hydrostatics will allow evolving mass to be suspended so that as they emerge from the water will the strength in gravity evolve it's mass to be larger from needing more energy to work to fight the force to create larger humanoids through enacting in an increase in the metabolic rate to consume more food to thus produce a larger species so a balance can occur between respiration and the metabolism from cellular respiration to fight the force as one moves so that as size increases it will have us move faster from our strength so a mile's hike will feel the same on both planets. Smaller planets would produce smaller humanoids despite genetics being relative per planet.

The Universe pulled consciousness into being(form). From a nature of basic stimulosus to have us fight or flee, to the brain that can think dimensionally. Amongst all the species of mammals our genetics were just right to have the brain grow to be as large as it is so that self awareness, reasoning, and dimensional thinking can take place.

Consciousness equals awareness, and is the last part of the creation of our Universe but the first for God due to his eternal potential of energy/force existing that would conserve a potential of life through being held by the vacuum. Life and God would connect in a circuit t like lightning, as God's potential exist with souls that conserve life that is drawing a connection to it, however the lightning could be the soul from the potential of life uniting with the potential of God to place quantity in motion. The connection of God to the conscious is unknown to me but if God exists to conserve the potential of life than there must be a resonation or energy transference within plants and animals that would signal God. There would be a connection to the conscious but through a circuit like lightning(potential differences) as the body pulls on the soul and God's consciousness to unite with the physical body. The physical plane gives God his eternal nature from nature being born out of an energy dependant Universe to have God and the physical plane unite through nature but how his eternal consciousness would connect with the physical body to have us actualize the nature of the conscious is unknown to me.

Life is not born out and from Chaos but Chaos will remain Ordered as Order rises through the creation of life adding force to the Universe and creating the living conscious. Life increasing force within the dimensions of space as we pulled into time from a slow process of evolution for living mass had the recognition of Order rise from a system of growth so that from mass through force being added with time, Order will rise through being energy dependant amongst the Chaos of change(force) but from a force inequality with distance. Since we are able to have a definition for Chaos, it means that it's unpredictability and disorder has predictability and order within its measure or we would be unable to define it. Therefore, uncertainty has been predicted to show us that unpredictability is part of the Nature of our Universe to show us that there is an inequality within the system forcing change. True Chaos cannot exist or it would spiral everything into itself to destroy itself as it remains too unpredictable for us to know and therefore we wouldn't be able to exist because True Chaos cannot establish order so that we can live let alone have self awareness and form definitives on it's nature. We can only recognize Chaos from being a part of Chaos through the Order of creation that has unpredictability be part of a dimensional force inequality created by a volumetric dimension and energy that gave rise to the existence of nature which, oddly enough, such nature is one with God, as nature brought reason to the Will of his mind as symmetry ordered itself out of the Chaos of the constantly changing empirical world that naturally creates an empirical world that has asymmetry amongst an order of growth that creates symmetry. Virtue which are feelings that we attach to emotions is Order rising out of Chaos, as Order builds and constructs and Chaos is a falling apart, harm, pain, killing everything that is destructive that evolves from having to be energy dependant so that by doing harm are we doing it as a response to not having control but has us gain control through that behavior despite it following a falling apart that is one with the uncontrolled force of Chaos but gives meaning to virtue, as virtue becomes feelings that builds relationships and secures peace for the mind, body, ego, and soul which was created as we evolved through being energy dependant to have us use virtue to find food, have security, and find peace as lived to find an Order of security. Vices gave meaning to virtue as both fight the Way of Chaos from being an energy dependant form within a dimensional system so that despite energy dependancy being a part of Order for growth Chaos is felt from being within a dimensional system of dependancy. Virtue is for the growth and sustainment for the living body and the growing consciousness and vice is for growing through discomfort. Meaning, being deceiving, hurting, disrespecting, cheating in relationships, which has love be attached to trust, loyalty, faithfulness, respect, and honor so that when being cheated on we feel the violation of all those virtues at once, etc., leads to a falling apart and having to grow through changing our way as we get older. Virtue to live, Vice to make it harder and die which is saying that if we were untrustworthy, disloyal, disrespectful, etc., then we make it harder to grow to obtain what is needed to live. No matter what, Chaos is still present and cannot be controlled but True Chaos does not exist. Things cannot exist through destruction because destruction leads to nothing and nothing can exist in itself. It would cause that eternal imperfection to degrade into nothingness as a negative power that is uncontrolled leads all that can be into a state of destruction and nothing can exist from itself or in itself which not only means that if God were destruction or hate, life would be in a state of True Chaos and nothing could exist, but also the forces within the Universe would compound there force over time to destroy mass as everything degrades through pressure. To know that gravity does not compound it's force over time is to know that force is being stopped. Therefore, Order is allowed to progress itself through creation and not be destroyed by Chaos's force inequality but rather has mass come together as a response to the inequality to have growth emerge in an attempt to close the inequality to produce chemical compounds like genetics that increases force within the Universe over time to rise within the dimension of space by increasing gravity to be a part of the dimensional system, all to increase gravity to regain the gravity value from before the Big Bang.

Chaos creates asymmetry as symmetry rises out of the Order that growth brings. Meaning, because of an eternal potential inequality there will be asymmetry despite energy coming together to create symmetry. Growth emerging as a response to the inequality to close it, increased the inequality by increasing force as it gained mass but nurtured symmetry to sustain homeostasis despite symmetry existing in the nature of light within the mist to create a perfect circle in the form of rainbow. The light upon the mist shows that symmetry underlines creation but it is symmetry through dependancy of a working order to generate a harmony to show the perfect circle of light upon the mist in the form of a solar glory or show us the harmony that virtue possesses as symmetry's dependancy reaches all the way to the conscious so that we may be aware of virtue creating harmony and therefore peace through Order and glory through faith. Since symmetry underlines creation despite the asymmetry of nature from being from a dependant Order, we grow into perfection from symmetry underlining creation. We cannot grow into imperfection because imperfection leads to nothing and nothing can exist in itself which means that perfection is understood through symmetry and harmony through dependancy and God be understood as a Higher Order from the Mind seeing perfection in it's statics to know of a Higher Power through the Mind where all is Good despite living in a state of imperfection and being part of the dependancy of knowledge so that we may actualize the existence of a Higher Power through the conscious being a part of the working Order as God unites with nature through symmetry that allows growth and perfection. We cannot grow into imperfection but rather we grow towards perfection which is shown through the mind as we learn and rise upward in the conscious as the opening of the Mind is through understanding harmony and truth which brings symmetry into Order through understanding a harmony of life so that we may envision the perfect circle or soul despite being in an imperfect and asymmetrical plane. Therefore, symmetry allows perfection to be seen in an dependant empirical world that creates asymmetry and imperfection. This is done amongst an asymmetrical existence created from a force inequality unifying mass and the vacuum into a dimension to force change to create asymmetry for a Universal energy that is for growth, order, and symmetry from energies dependance. Love and knowledge which builds, as wisdom unfolds from your growth which comes naturally as you live and grow but most importantly as we think and search because how we think is how we see, will bring transcendental gifts like unconditional love, wisdom, and foresight, as our depth on life deepens so that as we use our wisdom on a certain situation it may carry with it transcendental gifts. Love and knowledge creates and does not destroy and is part of the Order rising from Chaos. Order rising through the human consciousness as we evolved brought to our awareness our behavior to see that virtue moves with Love for the love of virtue which establishes peace through the good that we receive from the virtue that we express that creates stability and empowers such behavior as we gain, as we live in a world of knowledge which, is always a living knowledge due to explaining the nature of the Universe that has made us be the nervous system of our Universe due to evolving from the mass distilled, to have knowledge and love combine for the deepening of the conscious and have a more conscientious life through the Order of Love and Knowledge. Since Order rises through a system of Chaos but we know that Chaos is ordered in itself, it can be said that Chaos is from the potential inequality in force that creation fought against as it evolved. This is due to energy dependancy for mass existing with dimension so that all energy possesses volume within the vacuum as the force of gravity unifies the vacuum and mass to have the force of gravity be generated from a three dimensional displacement of space that bends space inward to have the force of gravity exist in a gradient as it is generated to nullify a pushing outward of space with distance from displacement as a force is generated to keep the vacuum static with time despite measuring time through a dimensional work, force, energy with distance over time within the gradient field of space. However, because the vacuum is generating the force of gravity we would say the vacuum is not static as mass behaves as an inequality that effects an infinite volume from the inequality to have us say the vacuum has been changed and therefore not static. However, because displacement would be nullified by the generation of force, the vacuum's position would not change to have it therefore remain static despite generating a force to unify mass and vacuum to give us time and the relativity of time which is the nature of time's statics. The geometrical form like the Earth exists from force unifying mass and the vacuum so that mass may have a volumetrical form from mass being an inequality relative to the vacuum that generates a force to pull mass together but within the volumetric statics of the vacuum so that we can draw a straight line through the Earth to create a cubic volumes of equal proportions despite the force gradient. In theory, the vacuum would remain static with time despite force giving a nature to time and dimension despite actualizing it's static presence. From an existence of measuring energy relative to force to produce work to have us tell time, the force of gravity ensures that time exists but is static despite measuring energy over time. The Order rising from Chaos is from the potential inequality of force with distance that had the creation of life attempt to close the potential inequality by adding force with dimension to the Universe in the form of life but since charge creates energy dependancy to add mass through force to the Universe with time than a potential inequality exists quantum physically and dependancy gave rise to be a part of Order so that dimensionally we may exist within the vacuum and be a part of the vacuum's inequality producing force. We grew from the potential inequality in attempt to close it but the inequality keeps us forever bound to the cycles of creation, growth, and therefore time. Even though gravity creates dimension so that a two dimensional system can never exist which would span gravity to an infinite value as gravity nullifies the pressing outward of space through generating a force that would create a force direction where more space is compacted toward the mass but force is generated to nullify displacement, gravity would unify the vacuum and mass to have time remain static despite force having mass require a point of position to have force be applied to move an object. However, if dimension unfolds in an evolutionary scale then expansion of force would turn a third dimensional plane into a fourth dimension as force volumetrically unifies mass and the vacuum as gravity spans infinitely and instantaneously which from such an actualization we would have an eternal third dimension to be a static field before gravity's influence despite mass always existing to produce force and time eternally to have the time for space exist forever statically. However, because in theory gravity is generated by mass posing as an inequality relative to volumetric static third plane the vacuum seems inertial in order to create a reaction of force generation. Mass creating a potential inequality dimensionally through force to nullify displacement of space to draw forth the nature of time as time passes to give us an actualization of time's statics as charges displacement will generate a field to unify the mass and the vacuum to actualize time within an eternal static time within a static volumetric plane despite experiencing the nature(relativity) of time through force that brings us form to the dimension of the vacuum. If gravity does not effect the entire vacuum but instead spans to a distinct volume then inertia will be experienced the same based on mass beading in space and two atoms placed far apart would never gravitationally attract as they remain suspended which means that gravity would be generated not by the vacuum but from another source like with a magnetic field. However, because two atoms pose inequalities relative to the vacuum's volume than the generation of gravity would be instantaneous to effect the entire vacuum so that two atoms a mile apart will gravitationally unite after a billion years from gravity being generated to create an inertial state from the suspension of force securing the vacuum's statics with time as unification between the vacuum and mass keeps the vacuum static as force is generated to keep all in a fluid state of motion from the eternal inequality generated to always have a 1 exist within the field of space no matter how may zero's that it follows with distance away from a mass or atom. Because we can draw back time from the existence of a single charge generating a field of gravity to bring a nature to time despite generation keeping the vacuum static over time, then that means statics of time and space existed prior to the generation of force that is generated to keep the vacuum static so linear distance may hold true despite mass(density) posing as an inequality to bend the field of time and space. So, if gravity does not extend infinitely, a mass would gravitationally bead within space which would allow inertia and momentum but would give us a static volumetric vacuum on the outskirts of the mass but if this were the case than the inertial state of the vacuum which generates specific gravitational field values would create a boundary of gravity but this doesn't seem right due to distance existing so that the inequality in force will taper with distance as space(force) spreads to effect the entire vacuum to have time reflect an inequality with distance and therefore a gravitational attraction between atoms a mile apart. Even though the vacuum seems inertial from generating force as a response to an inequality in dimension, moving in space does not have the vacuum resist it's movement. Once gravity unifies the vacuum and mass in a manner where mass is not tied to the vacuum but obtains an axis, the mass if free to move in time. As long as force strengthens with time it is allowed to pass but if too much force is applied with time radiant energy will increase as it changes the shape of it's mass. Gravity being instantaneous allows us to place an infinite amount of force on an object and travel as fast as we want as long as we have enough energy to place the force as we attempt to move forward within the statics of time but be held back by the binding strength of the energy and how pliable it is relative to force conditions as it attempts to move faster than the rate at which it's energy can compensate for as if by tightening the foci through compacting space with time through force energy density increases as a response from changing logical points too quickly to have us change the dimension of our mass despite the harmony(resonance) generated by energy as a response to compensate for the force in attempt to conserve energy so that from an application of force it must be applied with time as the energy attempts to be neutralized by the force and radiate, as that energy travels over more space with time despite undergoing a decay(a breaking apart) so that no matter how strong the force applied, energy will pose resistance to generate a harmony(current) that places a time for energy relative to force as energy slowly breaks away instead of being instantaneously neutralized. So mass is inertial from generating the force of gravity and obtaining an axis from pressure upon a point from force pulling inward in all directions around the mass to have it remain suspended so that force is needed to move a mass from the stability given by the directional force which always remains spherical so that if there is a density inequality in the mass the vacuum will allow suspension despite the axis of superimposition placing an off-centered axis. The vacuum does not remain inertial after gravity is generated due to force ensuring statics so that it may move forward in time and experience decay or a change in shape from an application of too much force. Mass would not be tied to the vacuum under fluidity constants despite having acceleration limits be based on the energy density of the mass, considering the force of the speed of light is what a high energy density particle can obtain instantaneously to have a velocity of C and not accelerate to C to have the mass/light continually travel faster as time passes but for humans chemical bonding strength is not able to handle the immediacy of force. A human would end up spreading like a water droplet with those water droplets beading and spreading to the point where liquid will try to thin and start evaporating from the pressure of it's own mass under pressure to increase volatility and evaporate as if it is trying to release light from our bodies by spreading mass too quickly under high force conditions. Despite there being acceleration limits there is no speed limit within the vacuum. Gravity is ensuring statics for the vacuum over time in a manner where the vacuum remains in a fixed position so that one may pass freely within time's statics.

In theory, space/vacuum exists throughout mass, life, water, etc., despite mass having hardness, so the spacing between the nucleus and electrons held by an extension of force will have space(quantum gravitational fields) exist between particles. Force of a solid form does not trap space inside to be separate from the vacuum and displace space to generate a field of gravity that is only on the outside of the mass instead of throughout the mass from a gravitational superimposition created by every particle that the mass consists of creating a force of gravity throughout the mass like for humans, water, and trees. Force between particles is not confining space in a manner where it is separate from the vacuum. So that no matter how dense an object is, space will still exist within the mass and space will not be contained separately from the vacuum as we move and change logical points within the vacuum but rather would have that space stay one with the vacuum so that as we jog or move within the vacuum we change the field of space quantum physically as we pass through the vacuum to have gravity's constant bend space around the quantum particles to carry forward with it momentum from their inertial state. Even though the gravity of every particle is changing logical positions as we move to effect the vacuum, every particle is in it's inertial state from the gravity generated by it's mass so that as force extends within the vacuum it's gravity is not trapping space, so that as we move, every particle will slide over space when moving as logical points within the vacuum remain fixed. So as we move, the field of gravity moves with us to have us remain in an inertial state eternally despite changing logical point within the vacuum more strongly and more weakly in the previous position so that space will bend as we pass through the vacuum to give us the perception that the vacuum is moving through us relativistically as the points with the vacuum remain fixed but rather we are only compacting space/bending space and having it remain constant around us as we change positions. Our bodies are not trapping space inside us so that as we move we literally move within the vacuum as we quantum physically change the shape of space as we move to logical positions. Even though gravity is weak at the quantum level, the force from the electric fields creates space between particles to give us a volume of mass with space inside that mass so that volume for mass can exist within the volume of the vacuum despite the volume being a dimensional form to exist in the dimension(nature) of time and be one with the vacuum around it. Since superimposition occurs, it is most likely that the first force of gravity would be generated at a very small quantum size to establish a weakest force quantity possible to have it remain a constant so that superimposition can then occur to increase gravity within the field of space and create a black hole from a quantum gravitational constant creating superimposition. If Planck's length is the smallest quantity to represent a piece of a charge's particle than the mass posing as an inequality relative to the vacuum will generate a directional field to create a smallest gravitational constant so that gravitational superimposition may apply for the charge's mass and increase the force of gravity from the act of superimposition as mass or density increases. This way from a quantum gravitational constant we may have the Earth, Stars, and singularities from the superimposition of the quantum gravitational constant to give us distinct measures of force relative to mass/density. We are not tied to the vacuum despite mass being an inequality that generates force so that we may say an axis has been created and therefore resistance experienced from having to apply force to say mass is tied. The shear act of force generation would tell us that mass at a quantum level is tied to the vacuum so that from their force superimposition can occur to increase the strength of gravity despite the mass being free to move within a infinite volume of the vacuum that allows the existence of infinite force if infinite energy exists. So is mass tied to the vacuum quantum physically or is the force generation a means to unify the vacuum and mass to allow passage within the vacuum and obtain infinite speeds if infinite energy can be applied to give us an infinite force potential?

A singularity is like a heavier baseball. If you get a stronger person to throw it, it will travel at the same velocity of a lighter one which means that for a black hole it's singularity is not tied to the vacuum but can be moved when force is applied to have the vacuum move throughout it's mass as it moves. It is only the amount of force placed on all sides that has it require a stronger force to move it in it's suspended state. The strength of the black hole does not create a boundary within the vacuum only for the force of the speed of light to put a boundary on that of light to show light has greater mass through force despite it's energy density/mass remaining constant. All that exists within the vacuum must obtain dimension through force so that light may gravitationally accelerate faster than C as it is gravitationally attracted to have the greater potential of energy gained from light being accelerated be absorbed by the singularity so that the single photon will lose the greater potential energy to keep it's charge constant so that it can be remitted at the force of the speed of light which is not greater than the force of gravity, to keep light from emerging out into space. If the vacuum does not remain static as the vacuum creates gravity to unify mass and the vacuum than the force of gravity would compound to strengthen all fields as time passes and not be a specific force quantity that remains secure as time moves forward which shows that the vacuum is inertial as it generates specific force quantities as a response to the inequality to have mass fit a dimensional form and feel pressure as if the inertial vacuum is trying to conserve space by generating a force to conserve a volumetric static plane. Despite the dimension we live in being bent, linear distance remains true relative to a static plane of time and the static plane of the vacuum so that we can measure straight distances in a bent(dimensional) field of space and measure time from energy expended relative to the force(dimension) to measure how long it takes to get from point A to B despite time remaining static. It allows free passage within the vacuum as the force of gravity remains an instantaneous force that exists in a gradient due to the geometric displacement compacting more space with time the closer one gets to the mass due to a three dimensional displacement having force bend inward to a focal point which has force decrease with distance away. This is due to mass being the potential inequality relative to the vastness of the vacuum that mass is effecting through it's displacement so that as soon as charge/mass exists, it generates a force of gravity from mass being a potential inequality to create a gradient of force to the far reaches of space. So, as soon as space is displaced force is generated to nullify displacement so that from the existence of mass being an inequality it will generate a force as a response to the inequality to create the existence of time from dimension(force) and an actualization of the statics of time from a force gradient bringing a form to a static dimension. The vacuum pressing outward from displacement would be nullified by the generation of force to give us a perceptual compacting of space so that through force mass can fall through large amounts of space in a short amount of time to give us a perceptual compaction of space from displacement placing an inequality to have the force of gravity push that mass through that field of space as force nullifies displacement to have the vacuum remain static but volumetric and the falling mass will feel an inertial rest as it exists in free fall within a gravitational field even within black holes which means a spinning mass will keep it's spin as it falls but as it travels faster we would observe less spins with time to depict time slowing despite the inertia of the mass having it spin normally in time so that if there is a density inequality in the spinning mass the gravitational lock will not compound over distance traveled with time but will have that be determined by the revolutions of the mass falling in an inertial state. The vacuum will pose no resistance on the falling mass from compacting distance with time to have mass fall through more space with time compacted within a gravitational field. It allows an inertial free fall as one falls through large amounts of space in a short amount of time. It seems that even within black holes one will obtain an inertial free fall until impact or radiation exposure is met when accelerating with distance over time. Mass would not be tied to the field of gravity to stretch length of mass with time unless there is a fluidity constant like the speed of light attached to space time but since all falls at the same rate within gravitational field we would accelerate with our mass intact before impact or eradication from radiation as we descend. The proportions of our mass being within a black hole's gravitational field would be proportional despite our feet being closer to the singularity and having a stronger gravitational pull relative to our head but since it is a proportional gain as one's velocity compounds to be within the stronger fields of gravity for shorter periods of time then the head and feet would keep the same proportions of gain, there is not a countering force that would pull our mass apart when in free fall, the inertial state will not pose drag/resistance relative to acceleration from the force between them. Despite the force of gravity increasing as we descend we would obtain the same force proportions between head and foot within every field of space to have our mass accelerate in free fall and not be pulled apart. We would accelerate through our inertial state but if we were to put an angle to the direction of travel than the force between them will cause a pulling against the force from force between them as destruction follows until an inertial state is reached for the orbiting mass as mass pulls apart in the direction where force is strongest like sand falling in an hour glass from the force of gravity will the mass pull apart. Meaning velocity must increase to find an orbital velocity to hinder a pulling apart of mass.

Time moves forward for a black hole and it's singularity. The statics of the vacuum is secured by the gravity of every particle and together through superimposition does force increase with a masses density to increase the force within the field of space to have time remain static with the vacuum's volume. The force of gravity will spherically/volumetrically strengthen or weaken as a totality and not feel the limitations of gravity's ripple at the speed of light turn a two dimensional plane into a three dimension and four dimensional system through an evolutionary kinetic response but rather the vacuum and mass is eternally bound into a dimensional form to have gravity be an instantaneous reaction from being generated by the vacuum. The creation of the gradient effects the passage of time(energy, work, force with distance) despite time remaining static with the vacuum or change the rate of it's gravitational strength with distance in ripples at the speed of light. It is an instantaneous strengthening and weakening of force to an infinite distance to unify the vacuum and mass from nullifying a pressing outward of space to generate a directional force and not tie the mass to the vacuum but instead allows passage for all that exists within the vacuum as the generation of the force of gravity remains instantaneous and infinite in length to allow unification of the vacuum and mass so that dimension(gravity/force inequality with distance) will connect the two to witness the nature of time within the statics of it's existence. Even though mass is an inequality so that as a response to the inequality force is generated in a gradient(force inequality with distance) to show that mass is tied to the vacuum at a very small quantum level, the very act of a force generation would show that mass and the vacuum are unified but not necessarily tied to each other despite the finest quantum particle drawing forth a gravitational field so that superimposition can occur. Since we are not tied to force itself it means that the twins paradox would not take in effect. We would not age any slower or faster under different force conditions or traveling at high speeds. The fluidity of the speed of light being the limitations for the rate at which gravity travels would either have a static volumetric three dimensional plane exist outside the spreading gravitational field or the vacuum generates gravity so that the field extends infinitely so that the vacuum's volume can remain static. Mass does not fall into a two dimensional system, for even flatness of mass that we can see would obtain a force so that light may be emitted within the four dimensional system created by that force so that we can see the existence of flatness. No light would exist within a two dimensional plane therefore a two dimensional plane cannot exist. And gravity cannot extend within a three dimensional system at the speed of light because that would have the speed of light be placed on time which would be the warping of a three dimensional system into a four dimensional system at the speed of light which cannot happen because the warping of a three dimensional system has space time be connected through force to have a three dimensional system with a volumetric static dimension be reliant upon the existence of force so that dimension will exist under the limitations of statics and keeping statics secure through instantaneous change in the strength of force within space time despite displacement from a masses density being an inequality that the force of gravity is being generated to counter to have force represents a compaction of space with time as a product of the volumetric disturbance. If the speed of light measured how fast dimension travels that would measure distance with time to put a definite on time, the creation of dimension, and a speed limit, so if we were to trace back the ripple of force creating dimension back to it's source we would have no dimension and therefore no mass but since nothing can exist in itself something always exists and that something is energy/mass that will create a dimensional force despite the vacuum remaining eternally static to say something always exists but since we have cognition we no that energy will always exist and therefore dimension(force) will exist within the vacuum. This means the force of gravity would remain instantaneous so that if we were to draw back time to existence we would have the splitting apart of mass down to the quantum gravitational level to have dimension through force always exist to have time become an eternal actualization of time constantly moving forward without direction and not create a starting point of time and dimension but rather gravity will create an eternal four dimensional plane as the vacuum and time remain static. Mass has always existed and therefore a speed limit will not be placed on time. Energy/Mass is eternal which gives an eternal form(nature) to the vacuum. Therefore, the speeds of light is not the rate at which gravity travels but rather it is an instantaneous reaction to secure an entire static third dimension by the existence of force. Mass being unified with the statics of the vacuum has the vacuum's statics be superimposed within the dimension creating field of gravity despite force being created by the vacuum to ensures statics of a volumetric system. Light has dimension from gravity and therefore mass through force. All that exists within the vacuum must have dimension and therefore mass. The vacuum does not permit passage if one does not have dimension from gravity.

Traveling at the speed of light and emitting a pulse of light, the inertial state when accelerating would carry over to allow light to travel at twice the speed of light as the ripple of light in space time stays at the speed of light but follows with the craft at the speed of light to follow the inertial course. Since we are following an inertial course from traveling within a space, the amount of force from momentum will be felt by the mass to have the electrons of masses repel to create a cycling over as pressure is felt and met within a point in space as they travel forward in time so that more pressure(acceleration) must be applied with time to slide over a distance so the mass does not be destroyed from applying too much force with time to create an acceleration limit on mass.. This way sliding over the distance for acceleration with time, is a smaller length in time, and we will accelerate over more space with time as the time it takes to reach a speed wanted be measured by how long it takes to get to point B from accelerating and slowing. Since us people are at rest despite feeling gravity in the form of acceleration not from velocity to have the rate of acceleration give us a weight, than that means that within the vacuum one can continually accelerate but is needed in a manner where one must continually accelerate in order to feel the constant force of pressure which means the pressure constant has to keep secure by compounding velocity as we move forward and as time passes as we increase the rate of acceleration over time. If gravity produced only velocity than we would be able to jump up and overcome the force of gravity but because it is constant acceleration as time passes we have difficulty in doing so. If we were to accelerate it would seem as if the field of space tightens which is from that sliding period of compounding momentum and pulling G's from applying a direction of force and changing that direction as one turns. The force electrons have to repel against each other creates a sliding forward in time as we apply a constant pressure from acceleration to travel at high speeds. But as we release acceleration and coast at a high velocity we become particles bouncing in a box as we carry over our inertial state to have us move at sharper angles left and right in our inertial state without pulling any G's. Light would be emitted at the speed of light but carry with it the momentum of the craft to have light travel at twice that speed relative to an observer at rest.

Our bodies relative to time dilation regulates the work, energy, force of it's own body metabolically to not have time dilation age us, for we are not tied to the vacuum by gravity's dimensional force. In theory, batteries cannot regulate their work energy or force so when put under a weaker force condition the electron flow would be changed as if less energy is needed relative to the lack of force. So, when the field of gravity decreases the decrease in force will allow electrons to pass through the entire circuit faster as the mass of the system decreases despite charge force remaining constant to apply more pressure through the current to move time faster and have a light bulb burn with a stronger lumen quantity. So as mass decreases, the time differential of force decreases to make up for the lack of force so that by increasing it's velocity does the mass of the electrons remain the same despite transferring energy faster. We would conduct more energy in a shorter amount of time to have the battery decay faster but will produce stronger lumen quantity or increase resonance to have time pass faster. That is in theory anyways.

Light would move forward in the direction of the crafts movement despite it rippling outward at the speed of light. The statics of the vacuum would have light pulsate outward at the speed of light despite it traveling at twice that speed from an observer at rest in front of the mass. It would be from an onlooker observing the pulse of light to be stronger in front of the moving mass emitting photons at the speed of light but traveling at twice that speed to give us a blue shifted quantity of radiation as the craft approaches. Density increases as distance decreases with time to obtain an energy/mass/quantity from the added force from carrying over our inertial state from momentum to give us a dimensional quantity of energy in time despite mass decreasing as time decreases to give us a quantity of radiation from it's energy density. If a quantity of light measured energy with time than if a craft where to accelerate there would be less mass(photons) despite transferring energy faster as the force of the speed of light is carrying over a distance from sliding forward as it is ejected to have it obtain a greater velocity despite mass decreasing with time despite light being emitted normally from the traveling observer at rest. If the speed of light was a limitation to how fast space time warps, than at the speed of light, force would increase within the vacuum in order to keep the mass unified with the vacuum as gravity stabilizes a unification of dimension for the mass so that dimension can exist at the speed of light so that as velocity increases the limitation of the speed of light will increase force to keep mass relative to it's strength of gravity proportional as the mass attempts to force it's way past the fluidity boundary. A destruction of the mass would then occur at the speed of light if force compounded through a fluidity constant that changes the viscosity of mass at high speeds. But since gravity is a force generated to keep the vacuum static despite the vacuum creating gravity to establish dimension throughout objects down to their quantum selves to have mass feel the force from offsetting inertia as quantum spacing and movement of charges has gravity unify the vacuum and mass and would have any particle or mass traveling at the speed of light carry over inertia to depict a mass that is not tied to the vacuum under the fluidity measure of the speed of light that is causing a speed limit on mass. But rather stays suspended through the force of gravity not tying particles to the vacuum but is united through force for suspension to move despite repulsion and attraction of particles influencing how the mass compensates for the force from acceleration. Because there is a force inequality with distance then it is from displacement creating gravity to nullify displacement through the force of gravity so that inertia can be experienced in the dimension of time from an axis being established to show that mass is creating the potential inequality and therefore obtains a point in space from the generation of force over time to unify charge/mass within a volumetric plane as it remains suspended from gravity so that time(dimension) will be created from the generation of force as time passes from the inequality within the vacuum so that through force it will ensure statics of the vacuum but done so as time passes from force having to be generated to give us an actualization of time and therefore have time be based on force as time constantly moves forward without direction. A fluidity boundary is like throwing a rock in a pond, no matter how big the rock, the ripple will travel at the same velocity outward which when relative to space, the ripple of gravity will be at a constant C and no matter how big the rock that is thrown in the water, the ripple will be at the same velocity despite the wave having stronger amplitude representing greater potential at C but for time and space, the vacuum changes it's entire field instantaneously so that if we were to draw back time for gravity traveling at C then we have no mass due to the vacuum generating the field of gravity to unify mass and the vacuum which would leave us with a static vacuum and time so that if no mass existed time would still exist but through statics and if we draw back time from an instantaneous effects of gravity on the vacuum we would always have mass so that time will always be actualized. This makes gravity an instantaneous force so that as we draw back time we always have mass. Since the vacuum remains in a fixed position, held static, I tied time to the vacuum so that time would remain absolute within the vacuum's static and symmetrical volume because prior to the fourth dimension we have volume and therefore time through symmetry and statics to have time remain absolute/static.

Because we can draw a straight line in space despite the field of space being bent into a gradient, we know that the vacuum remains static despite the force curves but as soon as charge was created did time be pulled into existence from the generation of force to create the acquisition of a passing forward of time as force nullifies displacement so that one may exist within the eternal statics of time within a volumetric system. It is as if the vacuum is inertial so that as a response to a disturbance from a dimensional displacement force is generated to bring dimension(nature) to the statics of the vacuum and time which may have it's inertial quality influence the generation of a specific force quantity relative to the density/mass that is generating a directional field. It is as if both Newton and Eienstein were right, time is absolute but is also dimensional(relative) based on force, work, and energy. It just took the generation of the force of gravity to pull the relativity of time into existence to explain the nature of time and dimension through force that is within the statics of the vacuum as force is generated to compensate for an inequality within the system to give us suspension and an acquisition of existing within the statics of time but within a dimensional inequality.

Gravity would be ensuring the statics of the vacuum down to the quantum physical level despite gravity increasing through superimposition to have gravity's strength be dictated by density not mass alone so as mass gathers, superimposition will put pressure on the axis of the mass so that as mass gathers gravity will it pull together to force an increase in density as a response to the increase in inequality of mass that is generating a volumetric compression to conserve space for the inertial vacuum which increases thermal energy from compression at it's axis despite superimposition creating a suspension hole(point) at the axis of the mass which has mass at the axis be suspended as gravity pulls outward in all directions despite feeling pressure from it's mass on the axis. The gravitational pull point would be on the outskirts of the axis as if mass pressing inward is trying to spread pressure out over the axis instead of to a point. If there was a hole at the axis we would be suspended from gravity pulling outwards at the same time no matter how strong it is. So as density increases as the force of gravity increases the smaller and hotter mass like our forming planet becomes, to liquify rock and sink the denser iron elements to the axis of the planet to form a spherical iron core and increase gravity, thermal energy, spin, and rise the fluidity level of molten rock from transferring thermal energy over distance from the core to increase gravity through layering molten rock to decrease the volume of the planet and create an oblate spheroid shape from it's spin as the Earth started to expand as it cooled.

An object in motion will stay in motion until acted upon by outside force because the vacuum remains static and does not have gravity tie mass to the vacuum or compound it's strength as time passes within the static plane to have time always move forward through the cycles of creation and destruction. This allows time to be static with the vacuum despite gravity being generated by the vacuum to unify the vacuum and mass into a dimensional system to have us measure the mechanics of energy, work, and force with distance to measure time with distance within the volume of space as the existence of gravity creates the observation of infinite time from being within an infinite dimension so that the conservation of a static system will be at the expense of generating time from mass posing as a potential inequality of displacement relative to an infinite distance within the vacuum to spread gravity infinitely and instantaneously. This has all mass experience time despite time being held static as time moves forward. Because there is a potential inequality of force with distance created by the existence of charge/mass, gravity will extend to infinite distance within the vacuum as force is generated to nullify a pressing outward of dimension so that through force generated the vacuum keeps its place in time so that linear distance will hold true despite a colorful fluctuation of force existing within the vacuum at the speed at which particles travel as an instantaneous reaction allows superimposition to travel forward in time as being part of the totality of superimposition and not be tied(or be tied quantum physically) to the vacuum to have the vacuum seem to be vibrating or like a snowy t.v. screen with gravitational fluctuations. Because force is generated to unify dimension despite an inequality existing within it's field, the vacuum must be inertial in order to generate a force as a response to a dimensional inequality to create a current without extending or shrinking space to put a boundary on the vacuum and the rate at which gravity travels.

The creation of dimension would be Chaos's motion as the existence of energy/mass becomes a question on where did quantum physical charge/mass come from that Orders the creation of life as energy/mass pulls together down to the charges fiber and attract to opposite charges to have the reaction between chemicals under pressure cause Order to rise through itself to have us recognize the physical plane and the nature of the Universe that has created us. The addition of mass through chemical synthesis to add force over time in the form of life attempts to close the potential inequality just to increase the force with time within the Universe as energy comes together to have our consciousness grow if not pull itself out of creation as a byproduct of metabolism, mobility(all that is mobile obtains a conscious), and homeostasis despite the eternal consciousness of God having an eternal existence prior to the creation of the body to conserve an energy dependant nature within the Universe.

God would be a potential of energy/force that would exist with it's eternity as it conserves the addition of life with time within the Universe to have a quantity of life be measured by the density of the singularity and how much mass of life it can produce through the stage of Universe expansion to have life be an eternal quantity that souls would conserve prior to incarnation as the evolving consciousness becomes a connection to God that would connect with the evolving consciousness in order of intellectual capacity and it's self awareness as energy transfers from the living form to God to have the soul be like a conductor of energy from self aware organisms that would conserve the nature of the growing consciousness but since plants undergo cellular respiration they must have a life force that allows it to exist in time(dimension) as well as they add mass through force to the Universe and not from displacement alone but also produces oxygen which supports the existence of the living conscious, to have plants and trees be a part of the eternal conscious of God. This has all souls be a preordained quantity that serves as a conservative potential for life. Like stars that form from atoms but creates mass like iron to increase the dimensional force of gravity from it's density within the Universe, did life add force within the Universe in an attempt to close the force inequality that is forcing change with time and ultimately a re-gathering of the singularity's gravity by increasing density and adding mass with time to the Universe through having energy/mass unite to bring growth from dependancy to have us grow in an attempt to close the potential inequality within the system so that as energy gathers and creates mass(life) it does so as a means to close the inequality through energy dependance to elongate time to add mass to the Universe and form a dimensional unit of time to increase the field of gravity in an attempt to close the vacuum's potential inequality that the force of gravity is being generated to neutralize so that a boundary or bulge will not form within the vacuum from mass's existence so that force being generated to neutralize the potential inequality is neutralizing the vacuum to keep it static despite the force generation ensuring a volumetric dimension of mass at the expense of keeping the vacuum static. This is from thinking that a potential inequality generates a current but in this case force in an attempt to neutralize the inequality as force is generated over time. Life adding mass and therefore force within the Universe is part of the Universe gathering it's initial gravity value. A tree is not a displacement of a ton of water, phosphates, nitrogen, etc., but is genetically fibrous from chemical synthesis which is creating dense mass over time to increase force within the Universe.

Since we are the nervous system, the feeling and sensing mass within the Universe which blooms consciousness, we can say that all the stages of the creation for Universes exist for the creation of life. Self reflection and placing ourselves in the position of others through our empathy to have an empathic reasoning be based around the heart mind and of the ego but also through the body as we project self using the mind, are all a part of the nature of our conscious aside from virtue and vice which are conscious oriented despite them being feelings that change our behavior and perspectives on life and therefore being conscientious. The last part of creation for our Universe is the creation of the consciousness and a unification between the nature of the conscious of the living form and the eternal conscious from the soul and God.

Human growth follows like light from the Sun being just strong enough to help the plant grow, not burn it, has our consciousness evolve from a more peaceful species that grew into being territorial and dominant as we gained more control which had us start taking instead of sharing which included life and death. The very force of Chaos has us feel that we need control to live, which we do but to not have control is a fear that we confront as we grow and live amongst each other. This is why virtue is a light that helps us grow but as intellectual capacities grew did we carry forth the fear from having to grow in a world of pain as we learn, having to have in order to survive, and being territorial and dominant even through the ego to gain which leads to violence as we confront the ignorance of growth, all rose upward as our consciousness and self awareness evolved as virtue created from Order rising from the Chaos of creation that creates adversity, had adversity and Chaos give rise to the necessity of virtues peace as we grow which, strengthens consciousness and being conscientious. Our consciousness carried with it a nature created from the cellular respiration of the animal cell that exists with it's energy/mass existing within a dimension of inequality in force with distance. Competitiveness, territorial, virtue, all came from cellular respiration and from the existence of metabolic reactions but especially from our ancient cellular mass having mobile capability which is adversity due to fighting against inertia to move within dimension which increased our spatial awareness as we moved out of the statics of hydrostatic pressure that nurtured our the sensitivity of our mass and the force from moving against inertia and into a less dense field where force from momentum from the moving body is experienced more strongly, the growth of the brain evolved to handle balance so that our conscious grew into being more self aware from the senses following behavior of food sources to have us understand the dimension of our environment relative to self. Since Chaos is part of Order we can then say Chaos's uncertainty is a force inequality from gravity, oppositely forced charges uniting to create subatomic distance between charges, to have Order rise through dependancy to form chemicals through electron dependancy and then chemical dependancy to sustain synthesis so that uncertainty will always exist despite the Order within as all that is formed grows to close an inequality that can't quite be closed. Not only did gravity give us dimension but the existence of particles pulling together to create atoms that form chemical compounds to create genetics all the way to a multicellular organisms, had life fight against having to need and be secure to create hurt, harm, vice through ignorance and ego to obtain feelings of security and dominance to get what we want, peer approval, or power so that as we became smarter we became more tricky as if Loki was behind it, to have us deceive, hurt, and take, to get what we wanted but also had virtue and peace rise through consciousness to have us find a way where we can extinguish our feelings of insecurity or bad behavior as we live amongst each other through a more respectful way. Peace is old, violence is new. Violence and sex respected overshadows virtue from it's popularity to always be a new and fun thing from exploring the strength or sexuality of the form or feelings of satisfaction through the ego as violence is inflicted as we grow into being more mature. Virtue is old. It is from basic stimulosus to create early motor functions to form decisions on what is good or bad to create instincts from repetitive behavior to have us avoid that which is bad as we found food, avoided harm, heat, or cold so that through evolution it made us virtuous to survive as we lived in relative peace as we lived amongst each other but we grew more violent through being territorial and controlling to gain more through our ignorance but also through our ego from our intellectual capacity growing but wanting security and control, to wanting power. Evolving from single cell organisms that did not eat there own kind had peace be very old despite having to compete for food. The bigger and stronger survived and multiplied from superior mobile capability not violence which had those that survived evolve superior intellectual capacities as if they were more fit. Virtue brings peace and is part of our nature. Virtue gives us what is needed. Be if you are trusting, loyal, and faithful, it will bring you what you need from the love of those virtues despite the struggles in life. The value of want is not greater than the value of need. The virtue you put in on life expresses that.

Order can see only so deep due to an eternal dependancy within a dimension of inequality to have us say Chaos is present within an Ordered system. Order is within the forces to a point where uncertainty must exist in order to keep dimension secure to reflect an eternal inequality and a system of constant change(knowledge). This would have the Order of creation that is being moved by Chaos pull on God's conserved potential of soul energy in an endless cycle through the evolution of the species and it's consciousness in an attempt to close the potential inequality forcing change. The Nature of the physical world gives God's consciousness and soul energy it's eternal nature that is why in heaven we are virtuous despite no need for the actions of virtue to exist despite the physical plane creating the feelings of virtue to have us live through the good of our nature. Virtue is part of our nature and is one with God through conserving the conscious through it's Way. Even though the vice and adversity give meaning to the nature of virtue to have us understand the nature of self from self being naturally virtuous, virtue is held by God, vice is not because the sensitivity of growth lays around the conscious and God is a conscious energy. Souls existing and angels existing tells me that God is conscious. Since buildings and trees in heaven exist then in theory the entire dimension of heaven would be conscious but that is unknown. Since I learned that God is eternal than that means there would be an eternal consciousness despite only proving in nature that Meanings exist eternally and statically and knowledge is gathered through the dependancy of the empirical world from being one with dependancy in our individuality so that as we gain knowledge we connect with the eternal meanings in our temporal state. This holds that the conscious is held in time from being able to actualize existence from being a part of knowledge and it's working Order despite being in a temporal state but the superiority of God's eternality is a mystery from a physical approach despite nature being one with God from nature bringing a form to the conscious. Actions in heaven would be from the heart of consciousness from all that is good existing to support the conscious which has us actualize virtue as being part of the heart of consciousness which means we are less dependant than we would be in life so that from a lack of dependancy vice will not be generated. This would be for the Order of Love and Knowledge. Gravity's force inequality with distance from gravity creating dimension and the force gradients existing for every charge, would be the force of Chaos that generates uncertainty with certainty to create an endless inequality in energy density or force over distance as Order exists through the existence of energy with force through energy dependancy that hinders decay rate through forming chemical bonds throughout it's growth. Virtue is from energy dependancy meeting dimension to have us feel adversity so that the meanings of hate, jealousy or all vices give rise to the importance of virtues meanings which are feelings that help us live. Virtue moved our consciousness upward through the stability that Order brings through the knowledge and care that is produced and passed down. So even though hurt, harm, and vice creates Chaos and a breaking down of matter, being an energy dependant form did we hurt and harm each other as we evolved which means the act of dependancy upon food and security came from an energy dependant Universe that has us feel the Chaos of a working Order as energy dependancy gave rise to the feelings of virtue through the mind, body, and ego as the Chaos of gravity's force and an existence of energy dependance has us feel a breaking down, hurt, and pain in a dimension of constant change. Order is for growth and Chaos is for destruction despite having to grow in a system of uncertainty and asymmetry to find the virtue of the form which has all that is conscious have virtue as part of their nature despite the strength of their animal self. Virtues are feelings which means God has feelings due to virtue being conscious oriented. Nature is one with virtue and is part of the Order of growth confronting the adversity of Chaos's energy dependant and inequality in force's existence which means that somewhere down the road quantum charge was forced into a dependancy after they were given it's charge's force direction to form complementary opposite particles from the direction of the charge's energy's alignment producing a wave function that would construct or repel from other charges which in theory all charge is made up of quantum particles that have both positives and negatives to attract to form a quantity to have those particles oscillate or align in a manner that shows a potential inequality exist within the charge relative to it's counter part so that between them there is a potential difference so that no positive particle will be positive and no negative particle be negative but be both positive and negative but with an inequality that is generating a directional current(wave function) to obtain a negative or positive force value. It is as if there is a binding direction to generate a direction of force for the volumetric charge. All energy has force so that very essence to an electron or it's counterpart must have all of it's quantum energy exist with a force binding energy together but must be done so where the same energy flips or rotates in a manner to support it's adjacent energies polarity in a given location so that a bind can occur to generate a directional force as a totality as if it is a kinetic response to an inequality forcing a direction of movement from an act of dependancy.

Theoretically, as the conscious evolved as we evolved, God's soul's energy evolved with it despite God being eternal to support the conservation of life within the physical plane as if God is a fundamental force of physics conserving the potential of life to have God support a time period of evolution. Meaning, a different type of soul energy fits the consciousness of the time period of evolution of our bodies and brains which means our soul energy took the place of a less evolved soul consciousness as we evolved further into the future of intellectuality, peace, through understanding the nature of virtue, and the ability to harness forces(technology) from our body being evolved enough to handle the dimensional thinking of the soul as the Mind becomes a connection to God through the soul but with a evolutionary nature of the conscious from the evolving body. How such a superimposition of the Mind can occur is unknown to me but to know that there is an eternal conservative potential conserving life, than the eternality of the conscious remains superior so that in life there is a connection to conserve it. But where the force/energy density of God came from is a mystery. Through faith I know that souls, angels, and God exists which means they are a conscious energy and since life is a potential in time the existence of God would be a force for conservation to allow the living conscious to evolve from a mass adding force with dimension but how God obtained his energy/force is unknown.

The Son of Man(humanity) exists as a time period of the consciousness and conscientious welfare for the race of man. Like the Greek civilization then the Roman civilizations along with Atlantis before them, tended to the conscious of man through philosophy that includes mathematics on the nature of celestial masses, the Son of Man is an illuminating period of the human consciousness that is moved by the will of man to understand the virtue of the living form. After all, the clouds around the Son of Man(humanity) dim our depth of perception through our ego or ignorance but as we remove the cloud by understanding humanity to find the love of virtue and the peace that it brings, our conscious deepens, and as we secure the health of our body and mind through virtue, it reveals humanity for what it is but in the light of peace and growth, not tearing each other down through teaching and learning of how cope with adversity through harsh measures like talking trash or getting into fights. To know that the Son of Man comes in a cloud which limits depth of perception is to know that the cloud removes itself to reveal the Son of Man but for humanity as a whole.

Just like taking the plank out of our own eye before we take the speck out of another's eye, when we understand our ego, ignorance, or being judgmental we find that we have been hypocritical, for we would not want that to happen to us so why do it to another, we slowly remove the plank from even recognizing how it got there from influence societally or some experience that motivated our behavior and as we remove the plank we gain depth of perception through our self knowledge so that we may remove others speck through teaching them how to remove it or just plainly helping them in life to increase their depth of perception. Thus, taking the speck out of another's eye through our depth of perception making life more comfortable and less irritating through instilling faith and hope with intrigue for those that you have helped.

Regardless of this, Order is from the existence of energy/mass that creates genetics and cellular respiration and gives us a nature of virtue and vice through being energy dependant which has the Chaos from the living forms vice be an act of not being able to have control so we act without discretion to obtain for oneself. Chaos is a breaking apart that leaves us with no control despite having Order bring us virtue so that we can obtain more control. Chaos exists from the force inequality that exists within energy and within the vacuum. An eternal inequality that would pull onto the existence of God which, has God be a potential of energy and force that exists to conserve the potential of life to force God into cycles of creation. That is why God is not present upon Pluto but is present around the growth of life. It would be to conserve the existence of nature and the nature of the conscious as it evolves. The eternal inequality would have the physical world pull upon God to exist despite God existing as a quantity of energy/force that is a quantity that would fill the Universe with only so much life as the physical world gives God a nature. Meaning, only so much life can exist at a time upon forming planets, as evolution spans Universally to create a potential of life, a totality of energy existing in time despite not being pulled into existence, as Universal consciousness of evolving species grow Universally within the middle point of the Universes expansion which may include both expansion and contraction lengths within the Mean so that mass within the Universe will gather density to the point where the strength of the singularity's gravity is almost re-gathered but mass is so far apart that superimposition would be weaker to give us a slightly weaker proportion of the singularities strength of gravity to have the suspended mass invoke a weaker field of gravity overall as the mass feels less of a gravitational pull as the Universe remains suspended. The galaxies moving at angles inward would slowly start to pull galaxies/ black holes inward to a different axis to increase volatility(movement), which has the creation of life exist as an eternal potential quantity that exists with a potential inequality forcing change that is having God attempt to close the loop of the potential inequality through conserving the existence of life as the creation of consciousness remains an eternal potential that unites with life as the force inequality pulls God into a physical existence but the inequality will never close completely which would allow the eternality of God to exist within the volumetric statics of the vacuum but be pulled into the dimension of time to have the creation of life exist as a Universal time period. God would be an energy/force that is contained within the volume of the vacuum to be held in time.

What came first the chicken or the egg? God's consciousness or the evolution of the living conscious? The living conscious is held by the nature of the animal self applied to dimensional thinking capability and it's self awareness relative to it's environment to divide species based on if they are planners and problem solvers, dimensional thinkers, or plainly sense oriented and how strongly stimulated they are to flight or fight as they rely on the limbic system for programmed behavior. An advanced species would obtain all of these qualities but be known for it's self awareness and dimensional thinking while other less advanced species would have thought be directed around survival but not extending it to the point of reasoning existence but being able to plan and remember instead of being primarily sense oriented. Since the physical plane gives God his nature so that we may be virtuous in heaven, his consciousness has a nature but since life is a potential in time it would hold that God would exist to conserve that potential to have God come before the evolution of the living conscious despite having virtue be a nature that Life and God shares as if they are connected by nature despite God being supreme from being for growth and sensitivity for the conscious. In life we would be exploring the nature of the conscious from experiencing the nature that is given to the animal form. The nature of life is the form and thought is consciousness. The form of thought is the nature of the consciousness. So, God's first thought must have been to conserve the nature of life and the consciousness to bring all to their Highest Good in the dimension of time and over a period of time through a dependant way. God's eternality would exist prior to the consciousness of the living form despite the living forms giving the conscious it's eternal nature. Since life adds mass with time to the Universe to increase force within the Universe and Order rises through growth to have us recognize that Order derives from energy dependance creating mass over time then that means God exists for growth and Order which means that the Order of Love and knowledge through understanding the virtue of the form has God obtain a nature that is pure virtue from not needing the nature of vice or Chaos from lacking control take precedence over his eternality which means that through a lack of control one's life can be destroyed and destruction leads to nothing and God would not exit because nothing would exist but since life is created through growth, God must be held eternal through the Order of growth's perfection around sustaining the conscious. That would mean all that which is attune to growth lives as a part of God. Love felt by our nature would carry over from love always bringing growth, as his self awareness moves with knowledge to support the existence of consciousness but with a divine nature. So, a potential inequality that exists within the physical plane holds God in motion to conserve life by the connection of the soul to have the substance/energy of God be held in an eternal cycle held within the vacuum's volume. Held in eternity through conserving a potential of life created with time and in time to have God like life, exist as potentials that connect, as one remains eternal and the other is held as being a quantity of creation with time. Two potentials connect to cross the boundaries of time(dimension) to create a current in time, to create a quantity/energy with time between the eternal conscious and the life form so that between the two a transference of energy through a connection will exist. Is this the Will for the living form through our awareness? And does the current have a direction or is it an alternating current to have the connection between God and man have God's mind influence our intellect as the body processes sensual data to have the body change directions of current upward to influence the stimulation of God to create a moving of the conscious back to the brain from the Mind and body connection as the body follows the Will from our awareness or is our connection to God simply to allow awareness? A connection between the body(machine) and an eternal consciousness? Since the conscious has a nature from the human body yet God unites consciousness than the connection between potentials would have the eternal consciousness draw forth the datum of the empirical form like is taught through the Gnostic faith but such a product would derive from the existence of the Will so that knowledge can be gained in our temporality from our awareness as potentials meet in time, as God remains an eternal potential, a conscious energy, or. . . the current drawn between potentials is a life force quantity. Is it the Will or is it the Spirit, where all meanings stay eternal despite the meanings existing individually in nature which has us find the essence of life to find that all meanings are unchanging but are set in motion through the nature of dependancy to have the Mind of God meet the Body of creation to unveil the statics of the Spirit despite the nature of dependancy having us find the virtue of the form to understand the essence/spirit? Since God is a conscious energy and life is a potential as well, then that always has me always divert back to the product created from potentials generating a current to be the living Will due to it bringing motion through consciousness and therefore part of the current generated from the potential of God meeting the life force potential of the Universe. But since God is a conscious energy than that means he has an eternal Will which would have the potential of life be a reflection of self before life is created to have all that can be known exist as part of the eternal Spirit so as creation occurs, it generates a harmony for the essences that are a part of the Spirit as creation pulls meaning into existence to have the physical world stimulate the spirit to create an Order(nature) to God's consciousness so that a form of thought will move the Will of God and build an evolutionary scale for the souls conscious which would reflect the nature(form) of the spirit. Living and sensing to give us knowledge would be a recollection of the Spirit as it is stimulated in a harmony to have knowledge help us grow and therefore conserve the conscious as we live in a Universe of energy dependancy but how his eternal energy was created is unknown to me despite writing through faith. But what I do know is that God and life are dependant upon each other and that is shown through God having a nature. Does that mean God is a witness to his very creation as he exists one with it? Through it? For it? Since God knew of the natural disaster that destroyed Sodom and Gomorrah than God must be deep within Nature to know of such occurrences before they happen as if God feels nature to be conscious of it's mechanical processes. But how, may remain a mystery forever. Gravity hinders light escaping from a black hole to create an illusion of a dimensional boundary, maybe it is the same with God, not with gravity, and there is no illusion. There is a boundary held by a force so that his ethereal energy stays within his field but since angels exist within our plane then the vacuum must support the concealment of energy to have quantity exist within the field of time. The vacuum would be permitting passage. So, despite his force holding his souls within it's volumetric dimension, God may also be within the field of time as physics somehow connects the two.

Since consciousness is a higher Order, life becomes the last part of creation for our Universe that pulls consciousness into being with a nature created by the evolving cell within a dimensional system. The Order of Love and Knowledge secures the conscious through virtue so that we may grow without the harm created from our nature having to suffer in order to learn. It allows a deepening of understanding to help a person as he or she grows to obtain a more healthy life from our conscientious behavior as it comes to us like a second nature despite it being the first of our nature due to every human being, being naturally virtuous. Virtue is only a means to bring what is needed and what is loved. A person does not have to be perfect as they live to have strengthens of virtues in their life but as we apply them do we gain even if we do not receive as we live from a more stable conscious through our conscientious awareness. Order will guide you through understanding your own human nature and how to control it through rising in consciousness which may have you gain a conscientious sensitivity on life as a reaction to further growth as if the conscious wants to be deepened and is reliant upon the stability that peace can be formed sensibly. So, Order rising through an energy dependant Universe uniting to not only form mass but increase force within the dimensional system to be a part of time through the creation of life and a rising in consciousness to rise to the Order of Love and Knowledge as Order remains for growth as Chaos remains a destructive force from having a lack of control within a dimensional system that has a force inequality, force a constant change, but also from complementary opposite particles uniting, to have us say that uncertainty exists because of dimension, a dimension of energy/charge and a dimension of space. Since there is a density inequality and force inequality within the Universe, God will always be pulled into existence so that we may through acquisition understand the Order of Love and Knowledge through uniting the form(nature) to thought(consciousness) to understand the eternal nature that is one with God.

Even though it is your will that steers you moved by your desires, God steers your life through your will to live a happier life, physically, emotionally, financially, and socially to live a life of prosperity. He steers us through our will of right thought, right action, and right speech but most importantly through our resiliency to accept what has happened in our life and having the courage to move out of the shadows of our mistakes onto a better way of life through our inner strength cultivated using self knowledge of how life has effected us and how we have effected life. In a way we paint the shadows as we grow and as we look back in life we see a depth of self as we gain a depth of perception on life which can be seen as wisdom. We must step out of our shadows that saturate our conscious and into the light of self knowledge to better our self so the colors of our passion that we paint upon the canvas of life will shine with luminosity of self knowledge and the shadows become but a dim reflection of what once was cast from the ego, hurts, or mistakes we once made out of ignorance or what hurts we may have suffered in the past. Everyone paints a masterpiece of light and shadow no matter who they are.

As we look back at our life, we see a masterpiece has been created that our lives were a part of. A colorful life full of choices and experiences moved by our desires and passions in life. The shadows of our mistakes or ego during those experiences and choices give depth to our life as the focal point of self knowledge brightens the canvas to display a love of life, a love of God, and a love for each other as we expressed our self. But also do our mistakes effect each other to effect each other in a negative way which challenges us to not paint within the shadow but rather paint around the focal point of our love and knowledge as we overcome the negativity we might face that has us make mistakes or effect our ego in a negative way. Fighting ego with ego is like fighting fire with fire which has us dig a grave for two. It is best to have an understanding on the nature of man so that a sense of humor can be grasped so that sensitivity of the conscientious person will not be too sensitive as we live in a ego competitive society. It is best to find the love of being trusting, loyal, faithful and have pride in your courage but balance that with an ego and mind that is open to knowledge and understanding so that what we create in our life will be around the Love of Virtue from the good that we gain from our behavior and not competing through violence so that our self worth can reinforce the values expressed. It is unnecessary in an influential city state despite population increasing to live amongst the many desires and therefore actions that the people have. Even though both good and bad behavior is from gaining in a manner where we avoid suffering as we secure our psychological and physical well being even through the ego, we know that all people live to obtain peace. All seek to obtain security physically and psychologically as they compete and obtain for themselves. So as population increases and we compete egotistically and physically to obtain for oneself and secure how people think of us as we fight the way of virtue, we adopt ways that will secure our self amongst many. It is as if we fight the way of virtue which is fighting against stability as we grow because of the familiarity of the harshness of our environment having familiarity breed contempt from the manner in which we gain to know how to avoid repercussions.

So, by letting go and letting God we do not focus on the shadow of our mistakes but instead know of them so the focal point of self knowledge will have us paint brilliant colors of the good we chose to experience from the good we wish to live from our wisdom of self guiding our passion to paint. All from letting go and letting God to paint a masterpiece of light and shadow upon the canvas of life.

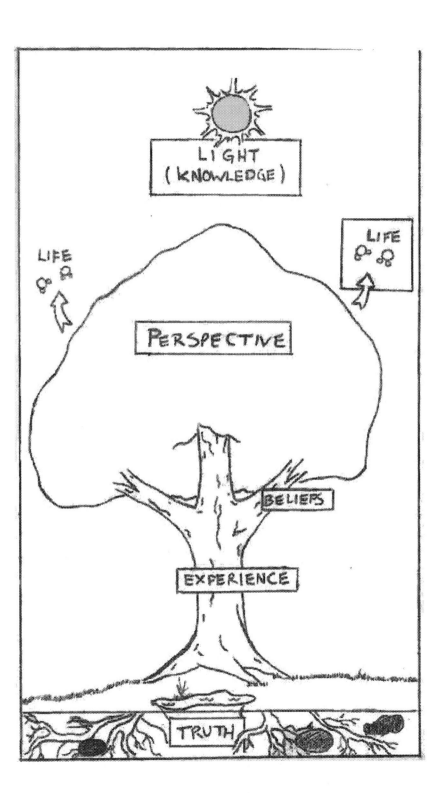

Perspectives, beliefs, experience, will, truth and ignorance, which are interwoven into living can be explained with the anatomy of a tree. The will of man is like the roots of a tree it holds him strong through life's storms. Through our will to live we absorb truth like water from the foundation of life which brings forth experience's. Our experiences then branch beliefs that sprout perspectives which absorb knowledge to give life in the form of wisdom.

The roots of a tree is like the will of man they hold him strong through life's storms. With our will holding us firmly to the foundation of humanity, we grow with the truths of life which strengthens our will as we expand through the means of self knowledge. Our will moved by our desires has us obtain through a way we believe is good and obtain what we want and need as we grow into a greater understanding. The truths of life flow through us as we grow and reach towards knowledge by expressing our self through our perspectives and beliefs which branch from our experiences. Planted by the will of our Father our will becomes his and together we give life to the world in the form of wisdom.

The truth we absorb is not only the reality in which we live but is from the conscious moving truth of intension, sincerity in action, and character that allows us to carry the nutrients of morality(virtue) from within our foundation(humanity) so with every decision we make as we experience self is made rightfully for the lives of others as well as our own as the foundation of humanity brings dimension to life relative through self. So no matter what we will absorb the reality of our environment to form truth but the truth for growth is the truth of life that carries the nutrients of rightful living. They rise with truth of good intension through the experience garnered. Such nutrients are extracted as virtue by our will carrying truth to have us live the truth as we garner knowledge and live a healthy and happy life through understanding. These virtues are expressed and felt as treating others as you would like to be treated, will power, live with knowledge, desires of peace, live with tolerance and compassion with understanding through unconditional love with an avoidance against the evils of man, the awareness to the truth behind man's actions which lay as intentions, do not judge falsely, never judge the soul, and love others as God loves us, selflessly with understanding towards others distress's. The truth we absorb in the foundation we grow we become a part of as we grow within our environment to effect our conscientious behavior as we carry the nutrients of rightful living to live a healthy life but we also lack nutrients from the lack of rightful living that is in our foundation which has us experience hardships as we strengthen our will to search for the truth of our foundation so we may obtain the nutrients(virtue) of living a happy and healthy life.

The foundation we choose to experience is the foundation of humanity. Families, work, school, society, our will has us make decisions. We choose to experience whatever is most desirable to us at the form of thought. Our desires move our will based on how to obtain and avoid suffering. We experience humanity and humanity teaches us how to behave. The foundation of humanity includes one's self so that by experiencing humanity do we experience the nature of the conscious so that the foundation of humanity stimulates us to effect our mind, body, and ego.

Ignorance in our foundation are like rock's because it hinders the absorption of truth which flow's rightful living. Ignorance makes life more difficult due to the fact that we have to strengthen our will to overcome our ignorance and move towards the truth in life through being open to knowledge. Even though the truth of life empowers us as we live a better way, the truth of life is also any way that we learned in life due to that behavior existing despite it not being good behavior. The truth to all is absorbed and is picked up through our desires moving our will to effect our behavior and therefore experiences.

Like the trunk of a tree that grows from its roots, experience grows from the will of man. Since we are all growing under different circumstances from the root of self, we absorb the truth of life according to how the environment is presented to us to have us complement it, giving us different experiences and beliefs based around our behavior and opens our perspective on life to have us see the world and obtain in the world in a manner that reflects what we believe. And through this do we obtain different beliefs all created from our experiences that are based around the root of self relative to our environment.

Our belief's branch from the experiences that have effected our decision making process to believe a thing is good and bad. Whatever we believe is good or bad is shown through our behavior as we gain in life. What we experience from our environment which, is family, friends, and society, we form beliefs on how to survive in that environment. Those beliefs are usually centered around self within the structure of society to obtain things for our own comfort but we also focus on the world and how our character complements the structure of society to bring society our presence of comfort. When our beliefs are healthy, making sure that everyone including our self will benefit from our actions, we make it a practice to treat others in a manner where they are respected and obtain what we want through believing that what is right will be given to us as well, through the respect we move through our faith. Positive experiences in the past will build and strengthen you to have you sprout health perspectives. The negative experiences will effect your conscious through your ego or through how your virtuous self was violated to change how you see life which can create bad way of looking at life but may also have you change your way of looking at life in a positive way. We live with tolerance but with discretion towards accepting the wrong ways of man so that we can have a discrimination against the evils of man but still have compassion towards them from caring about who they are regardless of their rights and wrongs. Those who believe in the knowledge and truths of life take every point of view that man has on life to heart and understands those views according to how his actions affect the world around him. It is always best to believe in a rightful way so that we can extend those beliefs through knowing of that way as we grow into using them to grow. It is best not to initiate in a harmful way because we know when that way of being dishonored, disrespected, and hurt do we have to struggle but even through changing the growth of our beliefs to grow out of bad behavior that in turn we would have to struggle with getting others to stop such a way in their lives. Beliefs turning into understanding as truth meets knowing as our conscious deepens as we grow into a healthier way will have us hold the same discretion onto ourselves as we know that we care about ourselves and use that discretion onto others. This way we approach believing not through gaining in a negative way but gaining through our good will. To have and to need, so that we can grow into having a more stable life of growth amongst the forces of nature and the force of man that we have to experience.

Like leaves that sprout from branches to absorb light and carbon dioxide to complete photosynthesis, our perspectives sprout from our beliefs to absorb knowledge to strengthen our will as we grow in the truth of self and learning of a better way. Our behavior in life, moved by our will, shows our perception on how life should be lived, as we believe in living a certain way that we have grown into. Singling each other out to being nice to everyone, our behavior in life is moved by how we perceive life should be lived as we gain and avoid suffering through such a way. Such a way changes our perception on life but also deepens our perception on life as our beliefs strengthen through knowing as we grow. An individual's beliefs shape their perspectives and influence how they see and create their world around them which, is bringing life into their lives. A clear perspective on life believes in how everyone including one's self can benefit from his actions and from the actions of others that he has influenced. They are open to the knowledge of life to promote growth so they may enjoy a happy life. The ones who have healthy perspectives and beliefs know that they are one part of humanity and not the whole body of creation. They see and believe as though they are but one ray of light in the lens of the eye of God. However, we all grow into this way, as understanding is reached but is known before this way is actualized through the virtue of the form. Virtue is the nature of the eternal form to have actualization of virtue be from rising in the order of consciousness from being conscientious as we look back in time to find that we are all naturally virtuous by nature. Feeling is extending to knowing from the seed of God's knowing existing as a part of us and creation of us to unite feeling with that eternal knowing so that our individual self can grow for God and into the light of God which, is also a light within us, though be it a truth within us, as the truth of the living body unites through a pervading knowing.

Deepen your perspectives on life so the light of knowledge may strengthen your life. Better yet step out of your perspectives and step into new perspectives so you may learn new and true ways of life that will broaden your horizons and take you on a kinder and more compassionate path in life to allow the conscious to grow. After all, one perspective does exist but many make up that one. Intent is moved by desire to have us be motivated to will our self to experience. Our perspectives is our approach to how we behave that effects our psychological and emotional well being as we gain and avoid suffering and what we believe through our behavior will show what we are attempting to gain be if it is peer approval or trying to gain peace which when placed in knowledge that behavior is learned and discarded so that beliefs may stretch to the light and have our perspective on life grow to be deepened as we find the true and better way.

We can easily say that our experiences are chosen by what we desired most at a time of action but were those actions chose in good faith and with the awareness of how our actions might influence others or did we not pay any mind to how we might be affecting others through our actions? We will all be faced with unpleasant experiences throughout life with situations and people rubbing like steel wool against our beliefs and desires, throwing us into an undesirable and stressful situations.

If we find our self in an undesirable situation we should ask ourselves what did we do and how did we act to bring our self into the current role we are playing. How am I being stimulated to effect my behavior or what is stimulating others? We may find that our motives might have been self centered, might have been through feeling hurt, or if we acted rightfully we could have been thrown into a situation where we became a catalyst to bring about a change that needed to occur. Experiences are experiences no matter if they are good or bad. During our life's experiences we should not only be aware of our actions and the actions of others during our experiences but we should also be aware of the role we are playing within them as we grow into a more stable and peaceful way.

Our will creating our experience as we rise towards the light of knowledge will our beliefs sprout perspectives which, are shown through our behavior so that the light of knowledge will be absorbed through how we are open to life, to show us how we have grown, and how we need to grow, as we shed our perspectives and grow new ones to strengthen our will as we grow deeper into self knowledge and extend outward to the world a more enlightened person so that we may give back to life in the form of our love and wisdom.

Through the lives we live let the beauty of the dawn rise from your soul, and the tranquillity of dusk set upon your heart.

!

Divine Rights

You have the divine right to be happy in life. It is your right as a soul to be treated justly, equally, and respectfully with the same love God has for us. We are a part of God and as a part of God you deserve this divine treatment from others. As you learn through life you will understand that as God is not cruel and vengeful for cruelty and vengeance is not a characteristic of Godly perfection only an action of man, you will undoubtedly understand you deserve to be treated justly and honorably as you treat others with the respect of the divine that you deserve.

Treat others as you would like to be treated:

Love as God loves, unconditionally, and with compassion towards others distress's. Remember that how you love others reflects how you love yourself.

Respect others with the respect you deserve. We are divine and deserve nothing less than the utmost respect. So in turn we should respect others with the utmost respect. And remember that respect is earned through honesty so that to trust will be strengthened. It is best to be true to yourself and be so that you may change as you grow older.

Honor those who show you the respect you deserve. Honor merits the use of respect so in recognition to those who a mutual respect is earned will they share between them the keys of life so they may pass the truth of the world onto the generations to come.

Trust in those who are worthy of your trust. For those who are trustworthy have a strong foundation of truth that they live upon and will hold your trust with respect so you do not get hurt.

Treat yourself like a God. Do not worship yourself but demand the utmost in life and how you should be treated by others and in doing so you will start to treat others as God does, lovingly, compassionately, without judgement for judgement is human alone, with knowledge towards understanding others distress's, and with the ability to discern the truth.

Even though we grow in life as mistakes are made by us or onto us, knowing that we rights that benefit the health of mankind empowers us. As we grow in the strength of God we should make it a habit to treat others as we would like to be treated, master our will, live in knowledge, search for truth, live with tolerance and compassion but with awareness on mans bad nature and with the awareness to discern the truth behind actions so we do not judge falsely, and love as God loves us, unconditionally. When we apply these truths to our life as we grow through good and bad we will become closer to God and live a happier life from the balance that we have obtained from our awareness of the way of God and man.

The golden rule is the cornerstone of love which holds what is dearest to the heart close to ones soul. Hold those who are in your life close to your soul and what is dearest to your heart will be expressed by how you treat them.

When planting a seed, what is required to grow a healthy plant? Good soil, water, enough light, and protection against the elements and harm. What if the soil is lacking in nutrients, and there is not enough water? Then we must get fertilizer to aid the soil, and find water to feed the plant. The same principle is with our lives. If we are raised in a society that is lacking the nutrients(virtues) that is carried by truth we will lack in the ways of rightful living. So we must find positive examples and mentors to aid our growth. We must find the spiritual food of knowledge (light) and truth (water) to aid us in our growth. A plant cannot live a healthy life lacking in the nutrients it needs. It cannot live healthy with the richness of nutrients in one area and lacking in the next. The plant needs a balance of nutrients. To lack in one area will bring about a lacking in another so we must aid all parts of the growth process by acting rightfully and keeping an open heart and mind through our virtue so we may lead a healthy life through striving to live a healthier and a more happier one.

Like plants we are different from each other. Some are big, some are small, some are colorful, and some are bright. We all grow in different environments and need physical and emotional supplementation of different virtues and emotional attention while avoiding access. From seed we have the potential to be a magnificent creation to reach the heaven above in a lifetime we just have to strengthen our will so we may strengthen our awareness by reaching for the truth of life so we may stretch our beliefs and shake loose ill perspectives while absorbing knowledge to not only give life in the form of wisdom but also live abundantly and healthy through our wisdom of supplementing our selves with right action, thought, and speech which expresses health. As plants roots grow deeper feeling for water and nutrients the plants grow bigger, brighter. The same is with us.

It starts with faith. The farmer does not know if the seeds will end up consumed or flourish but through his constant nurturing, he can make use his knowledge about the plant from his past experiences with them and turn even the struggling seeds into a prize plant. Be open to understanding so you can learn how your intentions in the past were indeed good intentions or selfish ones. Your intentions will bring a fruitful life or a despairing one. Prune the areas of your life that negativity has infected and supplement your life with faith, philosophy, thinking, and the knowledge of virtue, for when we bring together knowledge and virtue we have wisdom and when we have wisdom we have love that supports such wisdom from love moving virtue through our wisdom but done so naturally through our disposition as garner self knowledge. And it should be these that we supplement our intentions as we plant into life to live a fruitful one. You are a divine prize plant of God who wants you to grow and be healthy, so grow and start aiding your life with the nutrients of rightful living that God has instilled in you as your soul, so you can build and live a happier life. God has supplied us with the nutrients to live a healthy life we just have to use them through our awareness of them to deepen our depth of perception to gain a clearer way of thinking.

If you dislike your life, change it. The sooner you do the sooner the change in your life for the better. When a farmer plants seeds in a field, he plant's as soon as he can to use as much light as possible so he can reap a bountiful crop. He nurtures the seedlings to maturity constantly feeding them and supplying them with nutrients to increase its yield and when the time is right he harvests. Then the farmer prepares for the next crop to be planted. The farmer is constantly moving and by this constant movement, and faith, putting one foot in front of the other he will have a perpetual never-ending harvest. The same is in life. As God has planted his love and compassion in us that has started from seed and has grown through our devotion towards him, growing as he takes care of us in life we should plant him in our intentions. Start planting your good intentions and acts into the lives of others by changing our goals so we may change our life and live, eat, and love better than we do today. Sow good seeds such as virtue carried by right thought, action, and speech, into your goals so you will change your life and reach your goals and have a perpetual harvest of comfort, friendship, and love from the fellowship you find from others and well being you provide for your self and family.

To be an example of good is the fastest way to cure society. Good acts towards men are the hands of truth that has its tenderness of touch move the heart closer to the mind.

Being dependent on the ego is much like running out of food after over feeding a lion; it is liable to attack even his own master. If the lion would be patient and not give in to its temptation, he would never have to worry about not eating again because of his generous masters compassion. Feeding our ego sets an expectancy that cannot be filled and when there is not a source to fulfill one's want we end up hurting those around us to the point of our own destruction.

Knowledge is not a curse only a blessing and those who think ignorance is bliss and stepping back is a way to step forward will only find themselves back at square one.

Through life we will be compassionate to others as we grow with love for the world and for God. On everything we put our hand to we will put every ounce of what God has instilled in us. As his beauty flows through us we will live as it is our last day, as it is our first day, and as every day is for God. As we awaken to a new a day and to new thoughts let's thank God for what we know, what we will soon know, and give everything we have in us for him, through each other.

A life lived by the ego is like a handful of sand that slips through the crack of your fingers; the ego has a way of making the good things in life slip through the cracks.

Nothing is perfect in a world of imperfection. Everyone lack's in one way or another so by accepting we have imperfections it brings us closer to perfection and helping others from our self awareness and our understanding of tolerance through knowledge and forgiveness. By learning tolerance in imperfection we learn patience in reaching perfection and are able to tolerate each other and our selves despite our flaws because in an imperfect world we all learn differently and act differently by how we chose to learn as we grow in life. So we are not better or worse than anyone else we are our self, each unique, each beautiful, each growing in the light of self knowledge. After all, we all wish we were on the same page in life but instead we have to live

Tomorrow is today in a brighter light.

We are all walking a unique path towards God crossing paths with others uniting as old friends as we learn about life. During the moments where our paths converge time is shared between souls having fun and sharing a unique piece of God here on Earth. The time we spend with those who walk with God is unique to any other experience in the universe. The time we spend with one another encapsulates a piece of creation that is unique to God. It is a snapshot between two souls encapsulating friendship and love. It is special that we are alive for God but it is also special to be alive sharing a unique piece of God with each other. During the time we spend with one another we learn the strengths, character, and truths of a soul that God holds so dear to him. Truths and strengths that God has entrusted us with to bring to the world. When paths converge, we walk with those who we hold so dear to us, towards God, showing one another the truths of soul that form God's ingenuity and compassion. Even by spending a few minutes each day with one another we learn of the truths we hold. We might not know it but most of the time we give our truth by doing or saying very little. Our presence is felt regardless of what we do or how many words we speak. So let us make the most of this life as we walk with one another towards God. Let us be open and understanding to each other so we may not feel so alone in the world, so we can embrace through understanding instead of feeling so alone through our individuality so the time shared with each other can be a snapshot of the friendship between two souls and a fellowship of the human spirit.

A spider weaves his web to catch what he needs to survive. After he works hard in building its creation it receives. If the spider weaves a web with holes its dinner will easily escape and he will not be as healthy as the spiders that weave a strong web. So he tries to weave a web that is strong capturing all the good things in life to help him live healthy and happy. But before spinning a worthy web he must know about spinning webs and the worthy effort it takes into such an endeavor. By learning from trail and error and watching other spiders build unique webs in their unique environments he learns. After learning his spinning techniques and watching his mentors, he gains courage and now wants to show the world what he has learned. So he begins. In thought his web is perfect. Even though it is his first attempt he thinks positively and sets his aim high thinking it will become the perfect web. With great fervor and anticipation he builds his web in the environment in which he lives using the different unique perspectives on web spinning that he learned from others. After finishing his web he sees it to be flawless. Stepping back from his web he thinks it is perfect enough to take his spot at its center, showing the world his efforts. Upon reaching the center he sees his web is flawed. Looking at the web from and outer perspective, he saw it to be perfect but when we looked from the perspective within he saw it was lacking. There were holes. Being a wise spider he contemplates the mistake he made and finds the good actions that were lacking from his perspective of spinning that would have produced a greater outcome. From his faith and determination in catching and sharing all the good things in life the spider changes his perspective so he may complete the form of his creation, completing his form of growth and knowledge. Changing his perspective would end up being the key to his success and a happy life. He then goes to the spots of his web that are lacking reinforcing them with his new perspective of knowledge and self understanding that he could only have learned from experiencing what he saw from the other spiders and his mentors, first hand. Creating a web that would end up catching all the good things, he hoped for in life, for him, his family, and the world.

Like the spider we have the choice to spin a strong web through our virtue using knowledge to catch the good things in life and live healthy or we have the choice to weave a web of holes and see the good things in life escape our grasp. The catch is, we have to learn the best way to weave our virtue in the surroundings in which we live. By learning through experience we are able to build a strong web according to the properties of our surroundings to catch our dreams. Without being open to learn of our self through our experiences, our webs will be built poorly, as we do not care of our actions and how they affect others. Trying to weave a web of ignorance and ego lead us to be wrapped up in our own lies and deceit creating a web of holes, letting all the good in life escape because of our lack of understanding. A healthy web is built using self knowledge so you may spread your good acts equally amongst men to reinsure strength of character and ensure a happy and healthy life.

When we apply ourselves and put the right ingredients and time into life we create a tasteful and attractive life. Through trial and error we improvise with the ingredients and spices of life learning to make a very tasteful and full life with none or very few flaws. Through life's experiences we learn to live a happy life.

Life is like a loaf of bread. If we use the eggs of truth, the sweetness of knowledge, the milk of compassion, and the flour of understanding as the ingredients to the relationships we have with others with the yeast of love to make them rise we will have a very tasteful life. We will still have to go through the struggles and tragedies of living but our conduct on how we choose to treat others will make our life and the life's of those we touch sweet and the bitterness of poor actions on our part will not hurt others and haunt our psychological well being. But, if we use the ingredients of the ego which is hate, jealousy, prejudice, ignorance, and superficiality to lead our life we will have a bitter and flat bread of life that we alone have created.

The bread in life is the relationship we have with our friends, family, co-workers, and others that might be in our lives. If we use the ingredients of truth, knowledge, compassion, and understanding to flavor our relationships, with love to make them rise we will obtain sweet and close relationships that has us rise together. By adding those ingredients we will create tasteful relationships and pass on our ingredients of a good life to others so they may create loving relationships with those they have in their lives. They will learn how to treat others well from our example so they may bake a tasteful life. We are the apprentices to the baker to one day be the baker. We are learning all aspects of life and how to live a rightful and fulfilling one. Jesus like God is the baker and we are his apprentices learning the right ways of life through each other. We become mentors to those around us and take on apprentices' who will learn of our recipes and techniques to a better way of life. Giving others a better life from the good will we give to want everyone to live a happy and healthy life.

Sometimes we think we have added enough of life's ingredients and think a good outcome will be produce but sometimes they don't. Through trail and error we add the ingredients of compassion, truth, knowledge, understanding, and love into a relationship but there seems to be something lacking in our creation. When we look back, we see what we put into a relationship with our friends or co-workers and understand how we treated that person and find that we added all the ingredients necessary but maybe not enough of them, just maybe we lacked in the amount we gave. If we bake bread that is bland or bitter then be sweeter. If it comes out dry and without body then add more compassion. If we bake and our bread turns out flat then add more love. There is no limit to the love you can add when making the bread of life. If your relationship turns out flat then add more love(heart) to the actions of your body that you express and your relationship will rise through your good will as long as you have it in mind. If you bake bread that is small and flat how are you going to make a sandwich out of it? You can't. So add more love into everything you set your hand to so you can sandwich everything you love in life between the good that you produce through your wisdom. We can hold anything that we love in life, our pets, education, music, art, the world, our homes anything dear to us can be in our sandwich of life. Sandwich what you hold dearest to you between the compassion, truth, knowledge, understanding, and love that have created a full relationship and a happy life for you and all those who are in your life and you will not only enjoy a fun and fulfilling life but will experience new things that you love in life that you may have not yet experienced. By baking spiritual and loving bread with those who are in our lives and into the lives of those we love we will combine all the right ingredients and create a full and tasteful life so together we will never starve spiritually and emotionally. We will find harmony in living with each other.

Sometimes when we are truthful and loving adding all the ingredients to bring about a happy life and a kind relationship, we get people who treat us hatefully and with bitterness. It is not that our kindness is not felt it is just that they are on a different learning level. You have instilled the ingredients of rightful living in them but it is up to them to use them. If they are not nice and compassionate towards you then it is best to move on with their names in your heart. You can show someone how to bake but it is up to them to learn how.

There will be some people in our lives that will treat us bitterly and hatefully no matter how much spiritual ingredients we put into a relationship. Be weary of those people. Those dark ones will consume and consume the ingredients and bread we make and spit it back at us as if it is not good enough. We need to be weary not to fall into their traps. Sometimes we'll think that our recipe of love and compassion was not good enough because the bread we made and shared has been stepped upon and spit back. We think that since it is being spit back and stepped upon it must not be good enough so we give them more of our love and compassion making bread that we think will satisfy them just to find it stepped upon and spit back time and time again. Each recipe with special and unique qualities that show our devotion and love will be treated as if garbage. It is a trap. It is not our recipe of truth, love, and kindness, that is garbage it is their attitude of never-ending want and the control they try and have over us that is garbage. Our bread is special, our bread is unique, our bread is divine. It is made from you for those who need nourishment and knowledge. Be weary of falling into that trap where we feel as if our happiness depends on the happiness of others. The wrong people will use that to there advantage and it is detrimental to your psychological well being. You are a kind and loving person who deserves the best in life and deserves to be treated with the utmost respect and not with distaste. What we put into a relationship is what we will get back. If we choose to talk trash, we will cause resentment and bitterness. If we lie, we will not be trusted. If we treat people kindly, we will find kindness coming back to us. It is our choice how to live our life's but remember that our intentions into the ingredients we bake into the bread of life we have to eat. We have to take responsibility for our actions and our intentions. We cannot discard a distasteful life if that's what we choose to create. The difference between life and a loaf of bread is that we cannot discard a distasteful life and a loaf of bread we can. You create the life you have to live so let's create a full, happy, fun, and inspiring life by adding the right ingredients as we live through our learning experiences.

According to the dervishes, a person may gain material things by the Sufi Way if it is to the advantage of the Way as well as to himself. Equally, he will gain transcendental gifts in accordance with his capacity to use them in the right way.

When one live's rightfully, he trains to be the Master of his will. He control's the cravings of his body through understanding what his body needs and not what he desires that have him move to extremes in his behavior as his desires become his addictions. He learns what he gets into to understand his addictions and desires to be better off from his experiences. He controls his thoughts through his willingness to learn so through his increased awareness his perceptions will be clear and correct and not be hindered through his prejudices. He has compassion for others during their struggles. He learns tolerance through understanding all are growing into the Highest good under different struggles and circumstances. He searches for knowledge and truth of the life around him. He is inquisitive into his actions so he may understand his self, so he may understand others while always seeking the perfect one inside of him. Material things acquired are seen to be blessings, as he receives and works for what he owns. When one lives rightfully, they learn every step of the way to overcome failure and mistakes by understanding the humanness of the living condition.

When we practice rightful living, our ways of life are beneficial for everyone including ourselves. We are not trampling upon what we plant under our feet, as we try and plant more we are planting ever so gently with the skill of our ability so what we have already planted will not be damaged or destroyed. We will obtain a loving and fruitful life through our loving and modest ways. The ways of rightful living combined with ones abilities and unique personality will grant him material things as well as transcendental gifts when his abilities are given to others. As we plant ever so gently, working hard, caring for all that we plant in life, we will learn about everything we care for and grow with what we care for through our knowledge and willingness to learn. And from our love and caring ways towards all that we plant in life we will be blessed with the transcendental gifts and the divine knowledge to bring forth what we care for so deeply in life into the lives of others, so they may enjoy what we have so passionately pursued though cultivated through self as we plant what we give to others.

Building a relationship with the one we love is much like building a house. The structure of a relationship, like the structure of a house, relies on its many parts to keep it together not just one. When the foundation is set for a house, it sets forth the building of the frame. The frame sets forth the building of the roof and walls. A door is then set in place so one may enter the dwelling and windows are installed to let in light.

Love is a house built by two. With truth at its foundation so that through our love will truth build honesty to ensure trust is strong as trust spans like beams and supports that make up its frame which relies on the foundation of truth to be strong as love grows. Respect is the roof which sets upon the frame of trust. Honor sets upon respect as the roof's shingles showing the use of respect and having faith and being loyal to the one we love are the nails that bind the relationship keeping trust, respect, and honor together as a truthful relationship is built from the care we have for each other. One part of the structure relies on the other for support. If one piece was missing from the structure, the relationship becomes unpleasant, cold, and will eventually collapse from the lack of care that went into its creation.

When we are truthful to the one we love, we set a strong foundation to the relationship on which to establish trust. The one we love will trust us and in turn as they are truthful to us we will trust them. If there is deception and constant lying, the foundation of truth will be weak and the frame of trust will falter because of the lack in truth that is needed to stabilize the bond of trust created from our love which will effect our loyalty. Respect relies on the frame of trust to be strong but with trust faltering because of the lack of truth displayed, respect will soon fall because respect relies on trust to be strong so that through our love will we naturally be loyal and respectful because of the honesty practiced. Honor shows the use of respect and falls with respect when trust lacks. Being loyal and faithful holds a relationship together when a relationship is healthy. But how loyal and faithful can one be when truth and trust are lacking with respect falling from a weak foundation of truth? Not very loyal. We can be the most faithful and loyal people to the ones who are untruthful and untrustworthy but by doing that we would only be holding on to a relationship filled with lies and deceit. If you are in a situation where a person is untruthful and untrustworthy be faithful and loyal to yourself by getting out of that relationship. Do not do anything to corrupt the sense of love you have for yourself and the Highest Good by holding onto a relationship that is falling on top of you. You deserve to be happy in life and to be treated with the truth and the respect that you deserve and you deserve a lot so get out of the relationship that might be causing you so much hurt and build one with someone who deserves your kind heart, courage, and compassion. Together you will build a warm and loving relationship from the respect and love you have for God and the love and respect he has for you that are expressed through you to the one you love. When a mutual base of truth is established, the foundation of truth will be strong, trust will be sturdy, and the loyalty and faith in the one you love will come naturally, holding the relationship together creating a strong long lasting minty fresh relationship.

With the basic structure built we only need now to fill in the walls to make them solid shielding us from the harm the world produces, a door to allow those within our care to dwell amongst our protection and love, and windows to let in the light of knowledge.

We should insulate the frame of trust with compassion forming walls of comfort to keep us from the stress of the outside world. Not walls to keep us distant from others but walls of compassion so those who dwell in our love may be held through its warmth. By being compassionate we learn patience and should adorn the walls of compassion with our patience by being conscious of others welfare despite the adversities they may be experiencing in life. The door to our house of love is our will. It is not only from our will to build that brings forth the satisfaction of creating a happy home but it is also this will that allows us to invite others into our hearts. The windows are built from our points of view and judgments whose clarity lets light through our minds eye. The clearer our insight is on a situation the more open we are to understanding others views allowing more light of knowledge into the lives of those whose reside in our house of love, increasing everyone's ability to discern truth through the light of knowledge that they become exposed to. The clearer our insight is on life the more we are attune with the way the world works around us. When our views in life are narrow, caused through our prejudice, ego, and self ignorance, we create windows' that are small and cloudy hindering the light of knowledge, having our ability to discern truth be filtered through our judgments and discriminations.

When we find that person, who complements our character we begin constructing a relationship. What we have experienced from seeing others in relationships along with what we have learned from our own personal relationships with others, and what we desire in a relationship at our moment of growth we use as the schematics for the entire building process of the relationship. Since we are not the only one who is in the relationship we cannot build entirely on our schematic of how we think a relationship is built we have to combine our ways we know how to build with the schematics of the one we love so character and abilities can complement and construct a relationship that is comfortable, so a balanced relationship is created.

We are all lacking in one way or another and when we start building this relationship the strengths of one person will teach the other what is lacking. If one has a problem with trust, they will learn how to trust from the strength of trust in the other, as long as the truth in the relationship is still priority to keep loyalty from slipping.

Say both of you have established a solid foundation of love so that truth will build a sturdy frame of trust upon and one of you has had a hard time trusting in life. Then that person who is strong in trust will teach the other, if they are willing, to learn to trust. Its like one person knows how the frame of a house is constructed and the other has an idea but doesn't understand fully. So from the desire to build the house of love the one who is lacking is right beside the other learning and helping until he or she gets the hang of it and is now able to trust fully. Now if the one who just showed trust is struggling with being respectful and the student of trust is strong with respect the student now becomes the teacher. Together with their love and their desire to share this life and its beauty with one another they will build such a strong structure of love that their relationship will weather many of life's storms only to bring them closer together from the love and devotion they have towards building a relationship and a life with each other.

Both people must have that desire and love to build because it always takes two. If one assumes the responsibility for both during the whole relationship, he or she will get tired from the strain of trying to be respectful, fair, and having to do everything in the relationship. If we are out there, building this house of love through our will to have a good relationship, sweating, doing all the work while the one we love is taking a siesta in the sun or out messing around with others, criticizing us on how we are living, we will get tired not only physically but mentally because they're in this relationship too and they say how much they love us but they're not willing to take an account our feelings and be a part of the relationship or compromise on what is important to us. They would rather lie and not care how we feel and no matter how much we get them to try in the relationship it doesn't mean they will always be there to care and help. They might say 'okay, okay, I'll help, I care', just to find them five minutes later sipping back a couple of margarita's, listening to the 'Little Spanish flea' on the radio. No matter how much we try we cannot control them and make them be truthful, trusting, respectful, loyal, or any part that ties in with the structured relationship of love. If we do, they will only rebel and make it visible to everyone how mistreated they feel even when they're misleading's are the root to their misery. Eventually having the blame for everything that is going wrong with the relationship be put on your shoulders by those who sympathize with the one who misled you through his/her lies. Making the relationship even more difficult until we decide to leave or they leave us for trying to control them. Then why do they say they love us and get into a relationship when they're not truthful or respectful? I am not quite sure really. I only know that we cannot force someone to build equally upon a situation when they have no desire to. They may mislead us to believe they do but when it comes down to it they're only in it for their own comfort and not for the comfort of the one they love or for those who are involved in the relationship, like their children.

Let respect and trust be held close to your heart so that your love can bring warmth and comfort into your relationship. Making the relationship fulfilling and pleasurable, not seeming like work. The care for the one you love should be kept as a blue print to build your relationship and keep it strong and together you will have warmth as well as growth.

We should not mislead the one we love but instead be truthful about ourselves, our desires, and to our self so a solid foundation of love will hold a gradient of truth to keep the relationship both set and strong. Like with credit card companies. A solid line of credit, like a relationship, is established from being truthful and trusting in the promises we make. The more truth we establish by keeping our word and being honest in a relationship, the more trust we'll earn and the strength the bond of the relationship. With a solid foundation of truth built between two lovers a relationship will stand firm through many of life's storms. When a solid foundation of truth has been established through your love, trust will be earned. With trust earned we will earn respect. With respect gained we become honorable. And by being faithful and loyal to the one we love our relationship will be held together, with our points of views enlightening those whose lives we share whose names dwell in our hearts and amongst our love. The relationship with the one we love will be a piece of heaven on Earth. We will find that we have been truly blessed by God to have shared our life with the one we love and to have been allowed to share a part of their life that seemed to go by too quickly. So when you find that special someone, make every minute count, and do not take the specialties of sharing someone's life for granted because it is a great gift and a great honor to share the beauty of their strong but fragile heart on this beautiful gem called Earth. We should consider it a great honor and nothing less. We know how easy it is to hurt and be hurt and how hard it can be to unconditionally love and be loved, so we hold the strengths and fragilities our loved ones' soul close to our heart so we do not break theirs. In a relationship love is indeed a house built by two.

Life can be very hard. It can be confusing with how people choose to treat us, exhausting by trying to survive financially, and heartbreaking having to leave someone or someone leaving us that we loved dearly. It doesn't matter how much money or affluence we have, we all have to face the trails, emotions, and the experience's of being human. To sum it up, our life's experiences are extremely tough these days and it takes a lot for us to get through them. Those experiences, especially with unfaithful spouses, being discriminated against, or physically harmed or abused play on all of our emotions leaving us confused, desperate, and hopeless making any sort of escape seems like it is the answer to our problems. We try and escape our temporary reality or a past that is haunting us through drugs, alcohol, or even suicide from the daunting cloud that covers our hope and determination. But we can't escape those thoughts in life because our experiences are a part of our thoughts and no matter where we go they will follow us. We could even go for a walk or a jog and those thoughts will still find a way to surface. It just takes time, positive friends, and family to help heal our wounds through acceptance and forgiveness to eliminate negative thoughts to give us the strength to move on with our life and not fester in the emotional/psychological wounds we harbor like boats that pull self-loathing. Negativity from a past experience might have caused a deep emotional wound and might be excruciating with pain. But as time passes and your amongst positive friends and family the pain will slowly start to fade, the wound will heal, and you'll get an itch for living once more. You will still have the memory on how you got wounded and might be timid to get back out there because of the memory of pain, but the wound is now healed and you are stronger than ever before from that experience. Just have faith during the healing process and know that you have survived a tough experience and a deep wound that only made you stronger from going through that ordeal.

You are growing stronger now than ever before so have faith, courage, and believe that God is with you through the trials you endeavor to face. And above all believe in yourself. We seem to create the time to believe in everything around us except ourselves. Believe in your self. You are a part of God so believe in your abilities and truth as you would believe in the abilities and truth of God because there is no measure to God's abilities and there is no measure to your abilities, there is only the measure of time that makes us unable. The measures of man train us to measure our self against that which it feels suit us, like our social standings or personal disposition, and we never look any further than the measurement others measure us to. We should not believe in those measures but believe in the limitless capabilities we have as a person and a soul and stride forth to release the passion we have for life and God through our virtues, talents, and craft. To better our life, to better others life through good work that will build a stronger center and a rightful way that ultimately will give you pride in how you accomplish life despite how bad things can get which, means we should make every day count to our benefit.

We all know you are a very intelligent person who is a kind and loving soul and no matter what has happened in the past we will always know this about you so start believing in yourself as we do.

Through those troublesome times, center yourself and stop spreading yourself thin by keeping tabs on what it bothering you. Center yourself by writing your thoughts, working on your craft, and hanging out with friends and family. Get your mind off the negativity of your situation so you may work towards your solution by bringing positive things into your life. During such stressful times it might seem like there is no way to overcome the sorrow and stress you feel. Thinking you might not have a purpose in life or in other people's life. Stress is only confining your thoughts towards emotional pain or discomfort to direct your train of thought to be so self oriented that all that is thought about is the bad you convinced yourself into being from the rejection, ridicule, or bad comments heard caused by others ignorance or the mistakes that you might have made in the past that you eventually learned from that trigger you into thinking so poorly of your self. When in reality you are one of, if not the best person on Earth this day, for all is working to be their best but you have recognized your faults and errors as well as your strengths and achievements. We are here for God, for the betterment of our souls, for the betterment of other souls, and for the betterment of humanity that is a huge purpose and a great privilege. It might not seem that way during your most troublesome times but your presence is greatly needed and enjoyed. You are just caught in a difficult situation that you are forced to experience using all of what makes you who you are to overcome that adversity, to create a beauty and sense of balance to the world as you overcome your tribulations. Making you stronger and making all those who are around you learn from your strength and understanding despite them not doing so right away but they will.

I have come to an understanding of a truth that many have experienced and can relate to, simplicity is the richest of ways to live. It was not simplicity that made my life free it was the balance I found within my self from knowing my self and the simplicities of my needs, beliefs, and the hope of a dream to fuel a fire in me to succeed that made me free. I lived thankfully. I was nice to others, giving, and living in moderation never over extending myself mentally, physically, and financially. I lived like I could do anything which, was true because the only person who could stop me was me. And I dreamt. I dreamt of having a car, kids, and giving my writings to the world. And it became clear to me that I will have those things. Maybe not today or tomorrow but one day. I knew that those things would come but for now I had to create ways to reach those dreams. I knew I must keep one foot in front of the other and do the best I can with what I had so, I kept moving towards my goals one step at a time learning as I took on greater responsibility. Often failing but I kept trying. Much of what I write I have learned through experience.

Bad relationships, ego, vice, and being affected by others bad behavior at work and in society throughout my life which, I have found through my experiences with those poor choices on my part and feeling the effect of other's poor behavior it made life more difficult mentally and emotionally to reach my goals. I have been an egoist and I have lived virtuously. I still work on being in the moment instead of diligently thinking. I still work on trusting others. I have behaved rashly but have also behaved rightly which has had me understand the strength of virtue as I have found the value of virtue through my many mistakes to make my one day a reality. I feel I have made many mistakes and I am still working on my self and being a better person to this day. My one day hasn't become reality just yet because I have not given my writings but one day I will. I never thought I would make it this far and if you are reading these writings today I am closer to my one day than ever before. Just believe as you work and plan, and your one day will become reality.

One-day's become reality if you believe. Believe in yourself, your dreams, and your abilities. Live from the root of you and know that only you can stop you from reaching your dreams. Nothing is easy in life even though it is easy to become self defeating but if you believe, those hard times will not defeat you, they will only make you stronger and more determine to better your self as you move towards your goals of bettering yourself through bettering the lives of others. There is nothing we cannot do because there is nothing we cannot learn we just have to have the desire to know so we can learn all that we desire, as we have the confidence to relinquish our self doubt so we may take the time to learn because if we can learn what our ego desires to supplement our ego we can learn anything for the good of knowing so we may contribute our skills to live a better and fun life.

Go back to the root of you. Go back to that root of you who is innocent, kind, and caring, who loves to watch the clouds, climb trees, run and was always open to learning new things as we looked at the world in a state of awe and excitement. Go back to the one inside you who finds simple things to be so enjoyable and who truly relies on the conscience to live. That root is the real you. Not what others say you are or how they say you should act it is the God in you that cares for others and is giving to all and not only to those who you think are worthy of your kindness. That root is a root of truth and understanding that is your true self. It is your divine self. Get rid of the ego and the negative ways we were shown to survive like talking trash about each other in a negative approach and find that inner root in you, that inner child, and together we will live in peace and in fellowship.

We all start somewhere on the road to a better life, to reach our goals, and to create a better society. We start as bat boys dreaming to be the pitcher. We love this dream so much that we start by learning the game by getting out there and handing out the bats. By watching, learning, and experiencing as the team grows through the seasons we apply what we learn to help make the team a winning one. After the years of learning and applying we reach our dream of being the pitcher and are now the examples for the bat boys who dream to be the pitcher. A good example is never forgotten and lives on through the generations all from loving, learning, and applying.

God made man from the passion he has towards all that he has created. The passion and beauty that God holds for his creations welled up inside of him and spilled out to form all that which is dearest to him in the form of life. Everything he has faith in, everything he holds dear to his heart, has been created to live in the body of man to express his longings, love, and devotion towards the love of self and for creation.

Could man express the beauty of his creation under such negative conditions and immaturity of nature? God knew that the passion he had in creating man would arise out of man so man could live in the image of his creator. He had faith that the beauty he instilled in man could overcome negativity and be expressed. Everyday God sees us rise above negativity to express the love he instilled in us to the world and smiles.

He rejoices in seeing those daily achievements as we rejoice in seeing the good in God being expressed through us for others. God is proud of man and is overwhelmed with love for mankind, for man did not only live up to his expectation of overcoming negativity but he has grown increasingly passionate towards life and expressive in his love. Bitter as negativity is it has only made man sweeter. An effect God had taken to heart but could not fathom how far it can take man in his growth and his knowledge of creation. Such a strong force negativity can bring to express the true beauty of a soul and intensify the brightness of his spirt. When we lift weights, we get stronger and grow bigger. With negativity as a force that we push against we get stronger and grow brighter. The stronger and brighter we become the more positive energy we bring to the world and eventually the universe as we strip away all negativity that plagues are well being in life through our self knowledge of Gods knowledge. We are becoming the perfection of God in physical form to create as he creates and love as he loves and it is this that which makes God so proud of us all and holds us high. We are everything he wanted us to be and more and I am blessed as I know we all are to be his unique and vibrant creation called man.

Only in the ceaseless space of the mind can one attempt to fathom the distance God's love spans for us, for if one can dream of such a distance he knows of a love greater than himself.

When we look back through the life we have lived we see the world to be like sheets of music composed. On those sheets we create many good times and bad times scaling all ranges of the human condition. One thing no matter what has happened in the past is that we know that we have created a masterpiece that is unique to any other. It is this creation we must celebrate, and to encourage others that may take on what we have not yet endeavored to endure, so they may create a new masterpiece that will leave this place as beautiful, if not more, than we have created it to be.

The story of the Butterfly

Once there was a butterfly who wished she looked like the other butterflies. "Look at how they are adorned", she said to herself. " Look at the figure of their flapping." "Only if I looked like them, only if I were thinner like them, what if my wings are too big maybe then I would get more attention from them." So caught up with herself she did not see her beauty but only the appearance of others that she saw as beauty but not the beauty of who they were. It was as if she still saw herself as the caterpillar within the silk spinning before metamorphism but instead she was spun from her thoughts of desire, jealousy, or inadequacy amongst the beauty she perceived from not looking like all the other butterflies. Especially from those butterflies that criticize everything not like them. "Why don't they pay attention to me?", she thought. "Why don't I get all the attention from the onlookers?" Not even the people want to hold me. Then as she flew to the tulip she saw flapping but ever so gently, the most beautiful butterfly. The beautiful gently flapping butterfly looked up with surprise and saw the most beautiful butterfly she had ever seen and they talked and laughed as if they were old friends remarking on the beauty that they held. Then the butterfly went on her way happy as could be and the other butterflies who looked very beautiful to her saw her happiness and all talked like they were old friends. Never did she expect that they would talk to her since she looked different. Then one of the butterflies said, "you never looked different you were always one of us but never did you find happiness in the way you looked until you found that in yourself from the kindness of others. We were always kind to you, people wanted to hold you, but you were always flying away thinking you were never good enough. Do you now see that your flapping has opened up as well as your spirit? And with your spirit and your wings will you fly as far and high as we always hoped you would. Do you not see that we wished we had the beauty of your wings to have us fly with grace but we were happy in being our selves and how we were made as you have now found in our self. That inner happiness and self confidence is true beauty that accentuates your outer beauty because that inner beauty, that spirit, that confidence, that personality will never fade away. But just as important did you find your beauty. That butterfly you met was our mother and you found your beauty in your self from finding beauty in her from the confidence she gave you. Our mother always brings out our spirit, our confidence, our inner beauty. And it was your mother that gave you confidence in your self. We all have gone to her in our inadequate moments. We all like to be alone we all like to be amongst each other. We all think we are beautiful and at times we don't. You see, you always were one of us but we are all different like the flowers in the field and you found that beauty of self before you realized how beautiful you really are."

Even though we know that we have beauty, people seeing that beauty both inner and outer gives us confidence and pride in knowing that even though we are all different like the flowers in the field we are all beautiful with how God adorns us.

Poetry and story

Oh God, Father and Mother did you send me here? Oh world I gave all I could. No sooner in the blink of an eye did I lose my self just to find myself to be lost once more. Oh God did I fail you? But in my heart I was always there for what you have deemed me to be. Maybe in a dream awakening is revealed. Maybe in awakening is a dream fulfilled. But never did I dream to be awakened by a dream.

If love were but a drop of dew upon a rose petal I would say love is refreshing. If knowing that love was upon my heart I would say it is truly refreshing. But if my heart was broken and the love slipped between the cracks would I ever regain that refreshing love or would it fall to my soul for my roots to grow?

Tears fall like notes upon a sheet. A sound from the hearts yearning did it play ever so gently. Soft and smooth did they roll with the tempo of the beating heart as the composer trickled upon the sheet a melody from his life so sweet but bitter it made the angels fall. The tears wiped clean by an angels wing left the notes upon the sheet a mark of beauty and left upon the angel's wings a sign of glory.

What if we were like the drops of rain? Would we come together in a cloud to be a body of one? Would we fall together to be the body of lake, the pond, or the ocean? Or would we be suspended between bodies awaiting a body of one as we rise and fall together? Even though in the heaven do we unite and upon the Earth do we unite, do we make the choice of being one with each other throughout it all. I guess despite rising and falling the body makes us what we are as we rise and fall together as being one. Something that will always be.

Why is being lonely so difficult? Even when I found comfort in being alone did I still yearn for closeness. Even when I was around others did I yearn an incomprehensible feeling of being alone. But when I was in love did I find closure to the yearning of being one again. I suppose we always want to be one with God in life but have to experience our individuality amongst many individuals that are parts of the body of humanity that stretches faith, hope, and love. I guess through love did I feel closer to God.

If Hell existed for eternal damnation then every soul which is a part of God would be destroyed if sent to Hell which would be like God chopping off an arm and a leg and God is not a sadist. Every soul is part of the Body of God and God would not destroy self. Every soul is a piece of eternal consciousness(self).

If looked upon life like a child you will see magnanimity, wonderment, excitement, and fun.
If looked upon life like a man you will see lust, will power, strength, hope, and control.
If looked upon life like a woman you will see lust, compassion, love, and need.
If looked upon life as an elder you will see peace, stability, faith, hope, wisdom, and understanding.

If you combine them all, you will look at life through sustaining stability through your faith so that through your will power will you obtain what you need and hoped for as understanding and wisdom gained strengthens your willpower to have more control through the love gained from the peace obtained so that excitement and wonderment of life will fill you as lust stays as part of our nature that we explore. Compassion through understanding will have one gain an unconditional care to reflect a kinder nature of man. So, as we unify male and female through the traits of the young and old, time will stay a measurement of understanding deriving from an eternal wisdom.

If God intended for Eve to pick the apple so we all may live upon the Earth, I would build her a ladder so that she may pick the biggest and the most ripest one. Then I would build her a cherry picker just in case she likes cherries.

One winter as I was driving down the street I saw two people dressed in tattered clothes walking down the street behind the supermarket. In a glance I saw them embrace as I was driving by and together they shared a smile as she nestled her head upon his shoulder. Homeless or misfortunate they were no doubt. But that meant nothing to them at the moment as they shared the love between them. Oh, did I see the care in their eyes and in their embrace be if it was a few seconds glance as I drove by. And never did I believe in the power of love until I saw two people share a moment so precious to them when better food, clothes, and shelter was important to them both. To them they were the most important moment they could have in time despite the hardships they faced together. Sharing that time with each other is the greatest gift God has ever given us on Earth. And love became a greater empowerment than I knew it was and became even more precious to me as the water I drink, for both gives life even when life is hard to live.

When happiness was lost my dreams were joyous.

Always did I find myself in the trees, in the foliage, with the dirt playing like a kid who has found a new toy. Even the insects I fed and the trees I watered as I grazed on nuts within the trees and upon the ground as the ants scurried around me. The smell of life around me the sound of nature instilled peace within me. Always up in the walnut tree yards above the ground did I sway with tree as the wind blew. Caressing my skin and within my hair did I always enjoy the wind and always did I enjoy being a part of the tree even if only for a brief moment as I felt its movement when swaying with the wind. Wind storms would gust hard and rain would start to fall when all activity within the city was at a crawl and all the while I was up where no one in the entire city was, enjoying the tempest that Mother Earth gave to our city. Refreshing is it to feel her upon the wind and the water upon my skin as I exist for her within her nature. Always do I bring myself back to those happy moments where I alone in my childhood amongst a city of hundreds of thousands of people placing myself above the city to be apart of nature that not even a human can control. Ever since then I found the joy in the wind, the tree, the water, rainbows, and the lightning, did I eventually find myself talking to mother Azna upon the wind.

As the wind cannot be controlled neither can the people. That is why we govern our selves together as the body of humanity and together do we call ourselves a people like we call the wind the wind. We must control our self and in doing so we will learn to control others just by controlling our self. We are learning as familiarity breeds conformity so that we can all learn of a way to better our self through the stability that we create through each other which ensures health and happiness for us all.

Once, during a time in my life I looked at a tree and saw the glimmer of the Sun on the leaves and the movement of every leaf and understood that not one leaf moved in the same path that the wind has moved them many times.

Sometimes I wish I were different. Never truly content with whom I am, many times feeling inadequate about myself. But I find happiness anyway even with myself. I just wish it would be like that forever. I guess only in life do we feel that way, being human and all.

If I were a grain of sand would you write your name with me? If I were a grain of sand would I be a part of your castle? If I were a grain of sand would I tell the time of your life? If I were a grain of sand would I lay upon your skin? I was once a part of the rock that gave me my body but now I am with others who together form the beach of life waiting for the water to cleanse me.

Let it be in your mind and in your heart that you are special. Let it show through your body and show as you treat you and others well. Let life be enjoyable and enjoy each other. And never forget that we are sisters and brothers. Let you be kind, let your work be good, let you eat well, and let you be divine. Let you enjoy as much as possible but be well to each other and try not to be unlawful as you find a way to live, as you find a better way that you find contentment through. Through life it is all about being better and finding a way to be better despite going through what God has wanted us to go through as we fit the role as being a part of the sphere of human influence.

I am sorry for your suffering. I am sorry you went through the hardship you faced. I know it was difficult and is difficult. I know it hurt. Be proud that you are here. I know it is hard when things are so hard. But know that you have meaning and that meaning is why God put you here. I wish all of life was peaceful and perpetual bliss. Life is to suffer as it is to enjoy but know it always gets better. In between the good and bad find enjoyment and thankfulness for what you have and enjoy life through what you enjoy between the times of sadness and elation.

How Noah knew that the flood was approaching is beyond me. Did an angle tell him of the oncoming disaster? Was it a magi, a logician, or prophet? Was it Noah himself a prophet who had faith in things unseen and faith in what he saw in his visions? I don't know. But what I do know is that he believed and worked hard at what he believed in to save what he knew was precious to him as it was to God.

The destruction of Sodom and Gomorrah showed that God knew before we did as he sent angels to help the people of the city. And though it was nature that destroyed the cities through a built up thermal pressure as the sulfur and salts rose like steam and liquid to condense as they rose from thermal pressure, did chambers build underneath the strata to release a cascading explosion from the sulfur and salts. God knowing of such an occurrence and wanting to save the people showed the power of God and the love he has for us but it was through disbelief and a lack of love for each other that the love of God was not felt from not knowing God cared about them despite trying to help them. Sometimes if we care more about each other we would know that God cares about us and will help us even through each other. Did God smite the bad cities because they were bad people? No, it is from believing that God punishes did we interpret the event through our human nature of thinking God smites as we smite when all along he was trying to help through his unconditional love for all people. The destruction was a natural occurrence of tectonic activity and hundreds of thousands of years in the future the Dead Sea will have a strong chance of having a hydrothermal vent along the rifting diverge as the Gulf of Aqaba meets with Dead Sea as the Earth continues to expand.

Upon the pines the wind whispered to my soul that I am more precious than life. But it took the trees to tell me this from a wind that was the thought that moved them to speak. In thought do I think this was true but maybe the wind and trees never whispered to me. Maybe it was only my soul.

As intelligent and self aware beings that rely on being social and the need human contact we communicate through our self awareness. Competing for survival is one thing but the ego does not need to compete to survive it is their for us so we may connect with each other on the human level and be happy with ourselves, not destroy ourselves. However, such awareness through competing socially to gain has our carnality not care about each other so that we can have more but also keeps others carnality from hurting us. It is a way we all follow unknowingly as being man but as we grow older we connect with knowing that all human beings have been made to rise with each other and care about each other through our ego(self).

Soft they say, hard they say what do they mean? Gay, stupid. Ego behind words give approval or disapproval so that we will follow what others approve of to keep us from being hurt or away from the contact we need from each other. A way our bodies control each other through the mind as we follow each other to survive amongst each other. Strange, but interesting none the less. We are all human after all.

We are the most intelligent animal species on the face of the planet but we are the only specie that has killed the most of its own kind which makes us think, are we really that intelligent? I guess our intelligence is a blessing to have but when mixed with our carnal nature does chaos become apparent through our will and from how our nature is stimulated to survive, especially through attaching an importance of self gained through stimulating us to believe and then to act to any action to be the cause for the lack of peace.

A person who makes a person suffer who is eliminating suffering will suffer their self.

No human thinks they are weak despite having weakness but others focus on other's weakness to feel superior and gain an advantage. Yet to know your weakness makes you stronger but through eliminating all your weaknesses a weakness always appears. I don't know why this is logically? I guess it is the perfection in imperfection that exists in nature, for as the body of nature exists as being one in harmony with perfect strength. By being a part of that body we can be overcame by the forces of nature and even by each other and our self which is a weakness from being overcame by our own nature as being part of nature's totality.
I no longer bother with weakness and strength, for all people have both despite what the ego says. Knowing this I only bother myself with purpose as I cultivate self through understanding the self of God.

Despite having faith in things unseen or things we hope for despite not knowing if they will happen or exists in the world as being what we want them to be, faith is not in unknowing but in knowing of a greater power that works through us as our hearts are open to possibility. Hope, which is anticipation for what we desire to obtain in the future, exists through faith because our soul is naturally faithful and hope naturally occurs through our faith in God despite us not knowing of his/her existence or the possibility of God existing as we learn of God which means God has always existed through our feelings of hope because we naturally have faith. Through it all our heart is naturally open through faith that gives us hope.

Thank you God for the words I know, the words I can write, and the words my mind can form through experiencing your creation. To know that your words exist is to know that you exist or no words would exist to order what I know from your mind that has created everything.

Good and bad. Right and wrong. Beautiful and ugly. Positive and negative. Wise and foolish. Maybe all I can be is human and hope others embrace their own humanity so that humanity can be embraced by all and peace within the world can exist through social stability as self unites men.

Everything has reason. Even when someone says there was no reason for what they did, does the reason for their actions lay in not having a reason. Despite all having reason wisdom lays in what is right and wrong and our ability to stay right more often.

Sex is fun and healthy. I enjoyed it profusely. But now it does not concern me so much despite loving it. I guess I loved love which, made sex so great. Sex without love is like masturbation but more fun but it is not as enjoyable as when you love someone. Even though others might disagree, I think it is only our carnal desire of lust but also the relief of stress that sex provides without loving someone do we enjoy. But also from the connection with another despite love not being there but through the love we have for each other. But a good thing is that it's fun. Even though I do believe this is true it is not truly fulfilling. The look of love within a woman's eyes and throughout her body during sex is fulfilling to me as love connects lust. And as she looks at me with unconditional love throughout the day with her alluring stare and compassionate touch do I savor. If silk was as smooth as her I would savor such beauty. Maybe that transcends lust when a woman's heart is felt by a man through her feminine way.

What have I to give but only the eternal everything that fills a fathomless space within me from the eternal within me that stretches the fathomless space.

If I am so wise then why have I been a fool? I have been both wise and foolish. Through my foolish mistakes did I learn of others and how I got involved in such foolish mistakes and through wisdom did I not learn because I knew but only taught what I knew. So, even though it was hard to experience being foolish at times I have learned which I can't say I did when I was wise. I guess that wisdom is greatness and does bring peace but to make foolish mistakes only makes me greater than what I have been and is greater than what others seek to be for themselves when they do not seek to learn of each other through their own humanity as they extend their individuality to a totality through understanding totality and how to embrace humanity through embracing their own humanity.

Amazing how we learn through trail and error.

What is my favorite star? The Sun. Because I can feel its energy. Boring answer but true. However, there is nothing like the beauty of the stars above. They are truly amazing. Within a Universe of infinite proportion do I proportion myself amongst the masses of man, as the stars in the sky proportion themselves upon the human eye.

Philosophy is the root at which all sciences and religions branch. It is from the questions of why, how, what, when, and where did this root take form from our will. This will is a seed that sprouts philosophy as the human experience branches medicine, physics, biology, mathematics, chemistry, politics, governing, war, and religion amongst the many few that philosophy has grown into. We are all philosophers by nature of curiosity.

In this life I had a brother who was kind and giving. He is the best friend I ever had. I hope before the end I will be able to give him as much as he gave me despite him wanting nothing in return but a brother. :)

A mother was given to me both kind and responsible. The love she had for me was a rock that helped me gain stability even when there was miles between us. I hope that I may be a rock for others as she was for me as I give what I love to others unconditionally despite the love from a mother being more precious than preciousness itself. :)

If I were a ship my hope would be the sail raised by my passion that fate moves unyielding. But maddening is it when the doldrums in my life wreak havoc on my hope and passion from feeling I am going no where in life. I guess its fates way of making us work harder, be faithful, and never give up on the course God has planned for us.

I did not ask for what was given to me. Maybe in soul I did but in life I lived and experienced the world around me both good and bad. Religion was difficult because what is religion other than what the masses believe? And what was God anyway? War, peace, control or family, love, community or all of it. Society was difficult too much ego. Love was difficult, too many games. People saying bad things to me had me say bad things to them. People hurting me had me hurt them. People found ways to hurt for no reason or an excuse to do so. I had to find faith even though religion taught faith as I approached understanding religion through understanding why God exists through man's mind, emotions, will, and the words we have to express our self. I had to learn the good of society by understanding that we are all good by the nature of God's creation from all humans being naturally virtuous which, from experiencing the good and bad from both myself and others did my passion move me to write and in doing so did I release my potential. I found love and approached love from being a good friend and someone that would be there through thick and thin and found that love is eternal despite it being lost through temporality. It was the good amongst the struggle that made it bitter sweet despite me wishing it would be purely sweet. I learned words by the emotion behind how they were expressed to use them in a way that was bad when I was defensive as I learned those words from others and found that the only words that had meaning was the words of God, words of love, the words from the heart. And only from the morale given truth having me feel a sense of being one with humanity did I find words to be life giving, words to be inspiring, words to be uplifting, words to give to a person who is blue but has a heart that shines a light that is dimmed from sorrow or a lack of being given a compliment they needed but no one sought to pay attention. That in a sense made me, me. I found no good in being hurt and hurting. It is a part of life unfortunately. I guess through it all I learned and know that I was better off thinking for myself as I found a way to discern truth and live a better life as I sought to be there for as many people as I could. I guess people being there for me is what helped me be there for them and others. Without them I would not have made it this far. Especially through word. The difficult part was listening to others wisdom when I had it in my mind to learn myself. I guess from their wisdom did I eventually understand its truth so that from what I learned on my own did I find the empowerment that wisdom brings not only to my own life but to others. I sought after the truth. I sought after humanity being one. I sought to believe. And what I found was totality in being, a working Order of dependancy.

Knowing very little has me know so much from my willingness to learn.

Follow a way, a path that may have you lay stones for others to walk. See the stones laid so that you may through knowing of how my work or others were laid that will have you lay stones on a path created only by you for others to walk which, will give them stability through a stronger path laid. And from the stones I have laid may you step upon them and branch from them to give your understanding and unique soul and from what you have created will others lay stones on the path they seek to create as we create the many paths to happiness and fulfillment all spanning from heaven to Earth and from Earth to heaven to create one large road to happiness and strength as we experience the Pathos of life and extend our knowing through Logos so that Ethos will be achieved as we use our Minds along our walk towards God.

For a very short time I worked various jobs that needed me up and about early in the morning. Waking up at dawn working nine to ten hours counting the drive time. At the time when the Earth is lit in a dim lit blue a breeze from the east emerges in a subtle way. There is something so fresh about that breeze. Almost like the air is recycled as the cold air pushes to the west as the sun rises in the East. Even though I no longer wake up so early except on a few occasions I always feel pleasant with that cool morning breeze that is both refreshing and awakening.

The most beautiful sunset I have ever seen was while driving toward the west past Salt lake city by the great salt lake during early spring.

Upon the sky and the wispy clouds was there painted yellows, oranges, reds, pinks, purples, and a greenish tint that saturated the sky as light refracted within the wispy clouds. Never have I seen such a sight. And always do I know that God is a painter by heart of his creation.

In a dream one night I wandered within ancient halls with writing on a wall. I stopped to try to read it but it was in a language and carved pictures within stone I could not understand. Moving around and behind the wall I walked to the right down a hall just to have it turn to the left and right with other halls branching from the narrow and fire lit walls. I then found myself back at the room where the wall was and repeated the steps. A room I entered with a woman's face with octopus like arms moving in different directions but with a body round yet indiscernible. A game it was playing but it is vague to me if it was a chessboard on which I was standing or it was only a beige tiled floor? Puzzled and confused did I leave the room into the hallway picking up my step as to wonder where I was headed. Back at the start did I find myself in the room where the writing on the wall. Dimly lit was the room with torch. Within a wall underneath a small arch was a marble bust of an ancient with a wavy beard, wavy hair, and with a farrowed brow. Amazed I approached its fire lit face and remarked, Helios. And soon enough I was moving away glancing back at it as I moved to the wall with writing that was indiscernible to me and around into the hallway with a quickened pace saying, Alexander? Helios? With Helios in the back of my mind did I approach the room with the woman with many octopus-like arms but up upon the ceiling she was and I rushed out of the room and back into the hall where stairs visible amongst darkness were rising up in a wide Archimedes spiral. As I walked up the steps a gazebo did I approach but a helmet glowing of gold was before me. With great comfort did I pick up the helmet within mid air and put it on my head but I only remember me being before the gazebo upon the steps as I placed the helmet upon my head before I stepped upon the gazebo. Brilliant was the helmet. Almost a Greek bronze age helmet or Spartan helmet that was reminiscent to the medieval helmets of old. With a pointed tip, jaw guards, and a nose bridge did I put it on. But here I do not know why or how but I looked upon myself with head glowing from the hues of the shining helmet amongst a dark backdrop around the gazebo and stairs. Immediately did I find myself in another dimly lit torched room with an enormous statue of a warrior woman feminine but strong. A panther kept watch of me and approached as I jumped back not thinking if it was friend or foe. I avoided it and unexpectedly did it quicken its pace toward me and it froze in a grey stone. Their were large feline in the room but they froze as to see me but were stopped when approached drew near. "It must have been the helmet", I thought, but was not certain. I had this dream when I was at a very happy, virtuous, and spiritual place at the time when I first started writing. I never forgot the dream. I always felt it had great meaning despite not knowing what it meant.

Here before me a feather and wood. A thought in the night that serenades the stars amidst the wind within my hair, I do not feel the dread of the world or do not tread upon what fear that rests in guilt. But such peace that remains still not a piece of the world within me to confuse me I cared not for me through word but what I lived through word. I dared not to reason for what people thought of me but of what we all think but do not know. And there the feather blew in the cool night air upon the wood on which it rested was I set to write. Content, yes but why such peace when alone. I can't say I did not yearn to be with others but knew at the time I could not find the words to speak, the friendship to give, a woman to give to, or the money to spend. Alone. But with peace. Snow falling amongst the still night did I walk. Stopping at times to hear the snow fall. I thought of nothing. I was the only one. Walking alone. Cold never crept too deep as I came home to a warm place. Ahhh, God loved me. Warmth and food, books, a puzzle, and music. I was so happy. Work and home was the routine. Thunderstorms erupted in the fall and spring and there I was on the back walkway with clouds purple and pink, lightning flashed and burst. Cannons sounding next to my ear did my hair stand in the power of nature that I thanked God for. Winter was nice but cold. Never did I know cold until the bus ran late. Snow fell in huge chunks and blew to the side. Clothing not accustomed to the weather at hand did I wear what I had. I stopped feeling my feet but I knew they were there. Ice formed on my ears. I made it in to work but could not get warm so back out in the cold was I waiting on the bus. Ice formed on my ears once more. Walked home and what awaited me was warmth. Oh, did God love me. Summers were nice. Perfect. All seasons did I walk to see my grandparents. I stayed warm once I started walking despite the winter weather. One time did I walk in the cold to surprise my Grandparents with a visit. When I walked in, my Grandmother and Grandfather greeted me with a smile. My Grandmother asked me if I would get the snow off the back walkway and of course I said I would. Kind of hesitant I was due to being cold and not knowing why she would want me to do such a task because she saw how cold I was but of course I did. I didn't know the meaning of this but I swept off the back walkway. There in the window did I see my Grandmother look at me with a smile and I smiled back. After I was done I went up the steps and saw my Grandmother sitting there. Upon the table was there hot tea to warm me up and a cookie. My Grandmother just wanted to surprise me and warm me up like a Grandmother would but I surprised them before she could make the tea. That was so much love to me. She had a hard time walking but through the discomfort did she do that for me. That was very special. My Grandfather was just as special. Told jokes, laughed, and told me about the war. He helped secure Sicily in WWII. All my grandfathers served our nation from

Iwo Jima, Sicily, in WWII to France in WWI. And now I am here to follow the tradition in my family. Not through war but through peace so that we may understand prevention so that stability and peace can reestablish the way of working together through the values we share that we should rely upon so that we can stabilize health to rely upon what we need by valuing it to keep stable, economically, with families, and societally. Though it was through the mind did I work through reason despite having to experience many things good and bad to learn of humanity and to survive through the body which unfortunately effected my mind for the worst which gave me passion to change things in this world, so by learning of humanity through self did I learn of existence through feeling and learning the existence of words so that all people can understand through self and humanity so that we can understand the God in each other. Humanity did I grow to understand both in weakness and strength and sought to bring out each others strengths to rely upon so we will not rely upon each others weaknesses in the never ending popularity contest. But through it all did I start not liking my self or humanity but grew in knowing how nature has giving our conscious a nature that has us survive so that I could utilize the good nature within us to bring about peace through understanding life and God. Peace can come from war as much as peace can come from love but what we are dependant upon will have us strive for peace through what we know. Here before me a feather and wood. A thought in the night that serenades the stars amidst the wind within my hair, I do not feel the dread of the world or do not tread upon what fear that rests in guilt. And though I know of the sadness of men and women I know there is no boundaries to the God that I brought before me as he brought me closer to him and her.

If I were King of the Universe I would rule with the divine authority of virtue to cultivate a Universe of perpetual bliss with all children being taught to hold freedom of expression, physical, psychological, and emotional happiness gained through their virtuous ways a priority. To establish a free Universe that upholds civic virtue through people controlling their own will through virtue so that it may create a social and economic harmony for all people.

When our founding fathers wrote the Declaration of Independence they established laws inherent to all humans for all souls to express their self and protect themself. Freedom of speech, freedom of press, the right to bear arms, the right to trial by jury. But through establishing laws that would give this country a strong economy and military through democracy did they forget to add that we must not sacrifice other's psychological and emotional well being while practicing our freedoms. Not being a law but a statement of truth that will bind the fabric of democracy through the strength of social virtue that we have cultivated through being thankful for our freedoms, so from that statement it will display to the world that we are here for each other as much as we are here for our selves. Displaying the strength of democracy through the health of its people as we seek to gain through equal opportunity.

Through sincerity be with someone in relationships and business with a mutual respect so that your desires will build something greater for the two of you and hopefully it will be a long lasting relationship built on passion, goals, love, family, and friendship between them. With all built on grand intentions.

The word independent exists through dependancy. That is why we may be independent through our individuality and obtain health amongst each other due to being dependant upon each other for our well being. Relationships, at school, in society all are functions that we rely upon dependancy. Only when we hold strong to getting what we want through our individuality due to our lack of dependancy has us seek gain through harmful methods due to feeling we are not dependant upon anything. And even though we are always dependant even upon the way of our society that teaches us how to gain, it is gaining through a means that will not sacrifice our well being for the future through caring about each other today that we start caring about our future.

I hope. . .

I have faith in. . .

I believe. . .

I love. . .

I know. . .

I can. . .
I will. . .
Begins achievement, brings priority, and centers the self as one accomplishes themself.

Find moderation in everything but indulge yourself at times so that you can experience living. Moderation in ego, moderation in behavior, moderation in sex, moderation in spending. Find moderation in everything despite having and seeking plenty. But it is best to have moderation so more can exist over a longer period of time instead excess having us indulge over a shorter period of time. There must be balance for both as we experience life.

Believe me, God smiles as we smile. He cries when we cry. He makes love when we make love. He laughs when we laugh. He cares when we care. A living creation of God are we and he embraces our nature as a part of him, from his everlasting will.

A woman laughed and cried in the same day finding happiness in the midst of a struggling life. Always did she find happiness amongst her, always did she find something that would touch her heart but never could she not cry when in a world that struggles so hard to live. I guess she was only surviving. I guess we all do with hope that we will truly live one day.

I have been respected, I have been disrespected. I have won, I have lost. But through it all I realized that humanity is humanity and it will always be so despite others judging or treating us poorly for being both good and bad and right and wrong or by being us as we learn to live amongst each other and achieve through our way, finding a better one, and keeping the way that fits us best.

What is hell other than a state of mind, physical, and mental suffering, and ignorance that is for the Earth, for it is from having a body and vice to experience that puts us there and is created here from living with our human nature.
A man walked in the field with a child in his arms. Time alone they shared between them. And as they parted, for the man loved her deeply and she him, they both mourned each others loss. I wish things like that didn't happen. I wish we could always keep the happiness always and not only in memory. But the child kept the memory of the man's love with her and he kept the love she had for him and from between them did he keep a key to their hearts on the ring of his keys. She eventually shared a key of the heart but the man in the field, a father to her, shared a key of love and

friendship, a remembrance of the time shared between them. And he kept it ever since.

A soliloquy set upon the alter of fate spun with a golden needle and thread. A fabric of glistening words did it catch the light of mind and the heart it fed. Hues and tones did brighten as their past pains were shed and the soliloquy set upon the alter of fate became fate itself for those it led.

If not for the warmth of fire would I burn. Cold and alone the closeness of others left to yearn, that the stars above escape me. To the old and young they grow with knowing that they are free and warmth enfolds their belonging. Oh, so sweet does the fire burn as souls yearn, minds learn, and hearts churn so that no man will remain free until the fire inside keeps us warm enough to vanquish the coldness that keeps us from being one. And does the cold exist as a mass not from one but from many so as we live from the heart we will live amongst each other with the warmth of being one without the fear of being many.

A mind that keeps moving into the unknown keeps its energy for discovery. Especially when discoveries are made. The unknown cannot be so until we find why it cannot be and in doing so will we know that the unknown already exists as being something but it took a mind to find it.

I long for you dear. Here in this world where isolation has left me estranged from knowing you I yearn from knowing that you exist for me. The Sun rises and sets, nights creep cold, and wind blows, all the while knowing you are there in heaven waiting for my return. I like to believe you wait for me as I would wait for you maybe it is the hopeless romantic in me that has me think that. You are my better half both beautiful and divine and I will do what I have to do here before I get to see you again. Being away so long and going through it all I hope you can still recognize me. With love always, your soul mate.

If I were the Moon would you shine your light upon me? If I were the Moon would you use me to build? If I were the Moon would I be a part of your harvest? If I were the Moon would I turn the tide of your life? A body I am and use I have and I will always be there to affect you and even from the unnoticing effect of my force.

A key said to a lock, "what is behind the door?" And the lock said, "I don't know? I am looking out and I can't look in." And the key said, "Well, your part of the door you should know what's inside." And the lock said, "I am only a part of the door that holds what is within but I cannot see what I hold because I am looking out not within." "Would you like to know?", said the key. And the lock said, "Even if you tell me I would be unable to see it." And the key said, "Why not? You are a part of what you hold. You see that clearly?" The lock never saw his importance on being a part of what he holds as he always looked out to the world not within to what he held but it took a key to unlock the mystery that he was a part of what was within him, his storeroom in heaven. If the lock only knew the key was the mind that showed him that he was the heart in which his storeroom in heaven is unlocked maybe he the door would be open more often.

All that we acquire within our store room in heaven has been placed there through our good deeds acquired through giving from our right speech and action. From that store room do we unlock its treasure and give our good deeds, our compassion, our trust, our love, our forgiveness, our courage, our loyalty, our creativity, our talents, to others. Like jewels of ruby, diamond, gold, and emerald do we give love, knowledge, courage, and loyalty as we have it in mind to use our heart to acquire treasure in our storeroom in heaven through our good deeds and unlock the heart with the mind to give that treasure in life to each other. And often do other keys fit in our lock to show us the good within us despite not seeing it our self from others seeing our potential when we do not see it our self.

I wish I never was. . . I wish I was better. . . I wish I could only. . . I wish they would just. . . I wish I could have. . . I am just glad God is in control of our wishes so that he can make the right ones come true and not the bad ones out of depression, sadness, or anger as we live our purpose for him.

To be good at anything three things are needed. The most important is care. Care for your self and care to better your self and through that care will you extend from your self that care for others throughout your life, your work, your family, your passion, and personality. That care has you appreciate your work as well as care for your self as your self cultivation gives you empowerment to approaching success rightfully. The second is effort. It takes effort to learn and it takes effort to work but repetition is key because through repetition do we get a true feel of our work and it becomes easier as we seek to challenge our self. The third is determination we must be determined on accomplishing our goals as we seek to make time in our life in perfect balance with all responsibilities but not overextend our self mentally, financially, or physically as we make the time in our life to work towards reaching our goals. These three things are the basis for success as we seek the fruits of life and personal goals.

We must embrace our humanity both good and bad and right and wrong, for how else would we not keep us from truly accepting each other with unconditional love despite who they are as the body of humanity.

In my last breath I never thought. As my chest caved and eyes shut did I see once again hoping to see the stars and fire so that they may dance upon my eyes. Hoping to appreciate the beauty of life through the human spirit once more. And as the breath left my lips did it feel like a soft subtle kiss a repose of pain for the life lost both restless and tranquil. I guess we fear death because we love life and to have that fear is only because we love. I don't know why but I guess it was always love that kept me alive and not for my body but for my soul and for those I love.

God looked down and asked a man, "what is human?". "Well, . . ." the man thought, ". . . you must put the hue in human so I can know you through I so we can exist as being you or the I would not exist for us to know you as we exist together through self.

God looked down to a man and asked, "What is love?"
The man replied, "Love is what I want it to be." "And that is?", said God. The man said, "I love nature it feels fresh, clean, peaceful. I love people because they are fun, giving, and can be nice. I love women because they make me feel special, are fun, and they bare children that I love. And I love you because you are my eternal friend." Then God said, "You love because what you love loves you." "If I love hate", said the man, "does that mean it loves me?" Then God said, "That is correct." "But why then is love what it is when hate cannot be love?", said the man. "Because", God said, "Love brings what you want to you. It works through the Highest Good that is a part of nature that perpetually grows and through humans that is through virtue so that in which you love will be attracted to you. Even though love is my energy that is a part of you, your

bodies have want and that is from desire and from what you desire do you gain what you perceive is love. If you love hate then you desire it from feeling good from giving it and therefore it loves you in turn but only through desire, not the truth of what love is." "And what is the truth of love?", said the man. "The truth of love is me but is known through you as being unconditional love. Love is not from desire, desire is only a means to find love. Love is eternal and the truth lays in the connection that you have with others through your self as knowing me within you to love unconditionally as I do. "Is it wrong to hate?", said the man. "No its not wrong to hate but it is unhealthy to love to hate because connecting positive energy of love to that of hate is only having your carnal nature of blood lust that has lust be thought of loving hate but only because you have felt some good from others or to gain for your self through that means which have you rely upon it through desire to have desire be felt through blood lust not love. Chaos is then more apparent through your will through loving extremes but reflects only your want for power over others or a means to unite with others through that hate. That negative energy compounds as a group, as hate begets hate as judgement begets judgement to have judgement be a form of hate to bring such a unification through judgement create what would feel as being positive emotions from bad actions of judgement, so loving hate is only because your carnal nature is hurtful in order to obtain. Carnal nature is what nature has nurtured all living forms to have in order to survive and keep species from dying. Even though your carnality is often shown as being bad, it is also good due to your nature being their for you in order to survive. As your basic nature inflicts hate does it represent negativity but only through ignorance. Being man do you have the ability to rise above the negative aspect of your carnality. It is through the mind that you do so, as the heart and mind unite to have feeling fill knowing so that understanding can guide through foresight. Despite thinking that you are smarter than any other species, your carnality controls the mind when it is our minds that should control the body. This is difficult. Only because of having to go through the growing process where illumination occurs as ignorance is overcame but also because social behavior which teaches you what is right which can become a double edged sword. Through the mind through understanding will you rise above to a point where you may live as a man but divine through me. And from here does man love more because of the good he finds in life. And negativity becomes less because the knowledge I give has man find a way to love what is right through his nature to choose over what is wrong." "But what if I like to fight. Is that wrong?" "Yes and no." Your soul will know but you will cultivate your will through an honorable endeavor to be good at what you fight for or fighting physically to be the best. But to love to fight to make people a victim is using your ability to destroy the purpose I have given others that is equal if not greater than your own. But love to bring peace into your life so that fighting will not occur but only to protect yourself so that you can live my will." "So", said the man, "by loving hate do I bring hate upon myself and through my desires to bring hate to others and to avoid this I must love what is right but fighting is necessary for survival but to love to fight is only through honor to better myself not to do so to make people victims or gratify myself. But how will I know what to love is right?" God replied, "The good that you know is within from what you desire to have for yourself will you know because you know to treat others as you would have to be treated. Sometimes you will be harmed that does not mean it has been because you have hated or even disliked but because others are learning to love themselves and find a way to bring knowledge closer to their hearts so they can learn to love others and treat others as they would do their self so that they can find peace through me as they gain in life." "Do you understand?"

"Yes", said the man, "You are love and what I love I bring myself closer to you." "Yes", said God, "be more positive in what you say and do and through that will you bring the positive into your life just to find it was from your love that it was brought into your life as you lived according to how I would in your circumstance."

God said to a man, "You may not be given everything in this life but you will be given everything in the afterlife but what you will have in this life is desire. Desire is a good thing because wanting more is a good thing. Just do the best you can so you can do what you love to do so that you can give what you love to give. If you have to settle then settle but make money and find happiness with people and with things because I will always bring happiness to you to enjoy if you find a way to have them despite the stresses or hardships you face." "Just remember," said God, "do things for yourself to keep you going and find ways to do things for others and between the times of stress and happiness you will find peace of mind and heart through the peace you bring into your life. That is important to get you through in life."

God asked a woman, "What do you care about?" "Everything", the woman replied. God then said, "Do not care about everything that is unhealthy." "Why?", said the woman. "Caring leads to vulnerability. Vulnerability leads to rashness. Rashness occurs from being taken for granted through caring too much. Being taken for granted derives from being used. Being used comes from not seeing the signs that sometimes can't readily be seen because you care for them or something so much that you start caring for your self the least from accepting them and their actions from desiring them through your care for them to make them happy through being dependant upon them for your happiness. But most importantly leads to stress and depression from not feeling you are cared about enough because your energy is spent on caring but also from people not spending enough time to care about you in the same measure." The woman then said, "Then how much should I care?" "Well", said God, "care about virtue, that is a measure of how much care you should put into people. You might care and they may not. That is okay but do not put so much energy into something and get little in return. This means your energy is what they are using. Not to better themself but to receive from you. Caring too much has them control you through their will or sometimes through your own willingness to be controlled by them from desiring them or loving them. Together creates an unhealthy dependancy pulled from stimulating each other. For family, love unconditionally and learn to rise with each other and even if you fall, learn to be there through care. For others care through unconditional love but what you love, care about and for, so that it shows you that the value of need is greater than the value of want so that what you need which is shown through love will have what you love in your life for a longer period because it shows your care from how you treat it. This way your care will be moved by love. Care about what you love and show unconditional love and do not give of yourself to the point where you are being used. Your time and energy should be placed to bring what you love into your life. That you need for yourself to bring stability, peace, and fun into your life. And through this may you care for what is right and to care about yourself more than anything so that a measure of unconditional love will be drawn and be given back."

God said to Mother Azna, "I love you". Mother Azna replied, "I love you too but what about our children?" And God said, "Oh yeah, them too. I was just so drawn by your beauty my eyes wandered for a moment."

A very young child said, "Hey God look at what I drew for you", and rose the picture in the air. Upon the paper there were scribbles in blue and pink, circles, and triangles that looked like a cat. Greens and purples shapes and scribbles. And God said, "Yes, thank you. You drew a cat eating cat food after lunch on October fourth a few days after you saw him eat. You drew that because you love your cat. I like the food bowl and your mom sitting on the chair but she looks a little too round. The rug you colored is very creative keep up the good work." The child smiled and said, "Thank you God but you forgot the color was you, you can't leave that out." "Oh, yeah. . . ", said God, "I can't forget that, thank you." And God smiled proud like the crescent moon in the fall winking one eye as his other eye shined bright.

I know it is human to speak of others and joke in our groups, that is normal. But why extend words to hurt others socially because if those words did not exist we would reflect a stronger character. As we all know our desires move our behavior based on to gain emotionally, physically, financially, as our behavior reflects getting what we want or need despite intentions going unnoticed, so even though the human will wills to use words out of necessity or a lack of care towards each other, if those words did not exist we would be more positive because there would be one less outlet to express our lack of understanding or anger through a negative means to get what we want.

Micah said that mercy is greater than judgment. Mercy is greater because mercy is care and love that has God work through the hands of man. And from care and love do we express understanding to have us unite under values that may establish faith as a stronghold within the heart from faith working through care and love to the people to give hope to the people to better their lives so that their faith in themselves and in God will move their hope to reach their dreams and to a better way of life. Judgment divides people from people, religion from religion, families, and nations against nations so that as judgement begets judgement does hate beget hate to have judgment be a form of hate. Much like when stirring the pot who is the blame? The spoon. And when the spoon moves against the current it makes a splash to reinforce that it is the spoons fault. And so it is the same with judging. This has people see judgment to be strength despite not liking to be judged themself but do so anyway as what effects others will not effect them but because this way is carnal and establishes itself as strength do we get pulled into the drama that judgement unfolds as each others judgements effect our minds to control our emotions which then controls our bodies to place judgment ourselves. This then feeds our bodies carnality as we feed off each other emotions and comments. Despite nature giving us the ability to judge created early in evolutionary time to have judgement come before planning so we may know what is right from wrong so we can survive does our carnality compete through judgement. Because our bodies are strongly influenced by each others perspectives does our blood lust take over without discretion as we unite as a people to feel we have a cause. How can humans rely upon mercy when we feel people will keep doing bad? We can't know for sure which means that through judgement do we feel that we are doing the only thing necessary for their and our well being. We say mercy is for the weak not only because it is the weak that needs mercy but it will make us look weak if we show mercy. But also will others take us for granted as they see the mercy we show as being a sign of weakness so wrong can continue. It is much like having kindness be taken as a weakness. Despite this we should have faith and show the strength of wisdom for others and show the hands of God moving through hands of man by showing kindness to instill faith and hope. Through mercy teaching can be created through empowering them with understanding so that they may avoid the consequences of making further mistakes in their life to avoid the natural occurrence of judgment. This has punishment exist for those who uphold the law not by a people making themselves the judge and jury. Mercy binds the people through faith and hope as care and love is shown through understanding as long as we teach the values that may be used to better peoples lives. Maybe it is from the care we have for each other that gives greater empowerment through faith, through care, through understanding to have us care enough for them to have them bare fruit than to hurt them with judgement to hinder production so that it may send a greater message to the people through our forgiveness. Maybe the value of human life is greater than any value we have on want. And maybe by knowing we need human connection, the work from people, the happiness in knowing others are well, that empowers us to empower our self so that we can forever hold a value on the good we know we need as we reflect that knowing through unconditional love seen as unconditional care. Value on things through want should not be placed on the value of man through the judgements we have. It only depreciates the value of man through not holding a high value on what we need to reflect a kinder nature.

If work is like fruit that has value from what the people receive from it, why depreciate the value of the trees that bear the fruit. Would we be that unthankful. We would have the fruit, depreciate the value of the tree, and chop it down because we know we can get fruit elsewhere. The value of need is greater than the value of want and by respecting each other as we grow and live would be watering the tree so that it shall bear more.

Oh, do I know that all humans are growing to better their lives. And oh do I know that we will not always get along and some people will be bad at times and others good at times. But keep in mind and know from when you were in elementary school that when others did well, achieved, or bettered themselves despite if they had been bullied or got in trouble that we were naturally proud of them when they did good. We should keep that with us our entire life and not discard of that way as we get older. Have value on the good so that we may reflect a nation of values through how we choose approaching treating each other socially. The good is not as great if we use the measure of good to judge or hurt and not to be the morale in which builds the strength of the people through the value we have on human spirit.

I don't know what I would do if life on the Earth ceases to exist. I will enjoy it while I can. But I hope wherever else God puts me it will have the feel of Earth in its positive grandeur of both beauty, human spirit, rain, and energy.

What happened to the roles of women and men. Girls know not to hurt boys when boys are nice or the boys will hurt them and boys know not to hurt girls because they are sweet to them. But for some reason as girls become women they use men and play games and sometimes push them around thinking that men should accept it despite men being good to them and men hurt women by cheating and sometimes hurt physically thinking they should accept it when the women are sweet to them and both know that hurting is bad. What happened to fitting our roles as women and men and respecting each other for the care we give each other. Should we not keep in heart our inner child so we may know what the children know as we treat each other nicely, especially when we are treated well by each other?

My light shines. . .
My light shines. . .
My light shines. . .
My light shines. . .
My light shines through the darkness that surrounds me.
My light shines through the hardships that befall me.
My light shines through the love that is given to me.
My light shines for God and will not leave me.

The Crickets and the Frog

A cricket sat with a frog and said, "You sound horrible, got a frog in your throat?" The frog looked at the cricket and the cricket just smiled but the frog said, "Ribbit." The cricket started laughing hysterically. Then the cricket rubbed his legs together and made his music of the night and the crickets jumped to the cricket beat and meandered down to the cricket's violin upon his legs. The frog just looked at them all and gave a large, "Ribbit." Then a new cricket said, "You sound horrible, got a frog in your throat?", and all the crickets started laughing hysterically. The frog looked up to the night sky thinking, "Geez they sure can be rude", and said, "Ribbit". The crickets heard him and kept laughing so hard that their cheeks hurt and their belly muscles ached. And then in the most aristocratic and proper voice the frog said, "Oh, by lord do you crickets have a sense of humor. I have heard that joke twice within the hour. Talk about being a pain in the neck." And a cricket said, "Oh yeah, well I have seen your face twice within the hour and you have no neck", and they all started laughing uncontrollably. Then as the crickets laughed so hard as to be on their backs with their legs kicking with laughter, the frog said in his aristocratic way, " You laugh at me when you are my dinner? Well, thank you for the pre-dinner entertainment and thank you for the pleasure of dinning with me." Then the crickets stopped laughing and looked at each other and the frog just busted with laughter and ate all the crickets up. Satisfied he sat their fat and happy and gave a big and hearty, "Rizzeet" and said, "damn, now I have a cricket in my throat but its better than a crick in the neck."

Why was the father crab so crabby? Because he had crabs. :)

I saw a figure of a gnome peeing on a bush and thought that must feel good because he always kept that position. I guess we always keep positions we like or try to as long as possible.

When a blanket is gone all that we have is each other for warmth and to know this is to know that we should have humanity unite and care about each other so when all is gone or all is put a value upon, the value of humanity will not be depreciated from having bad experiences with each other as our desire for material things becomes the source of security that we rely upon as we struggle with the social stress we put each other through. Life can be stressful with bills and affording food, clothing, a place to live, and working but what if we treated each other better so the stress of the world will not have money be the soul source of comfort. Instead it will be the unconditional care and love for each other so we can release our potential and be more socially aware that we will find comfort in despite the stresses of life. The greatest warmth and security we have in life is being one with each other. This is a blanket that will never lose its warmth.

One summer I sat next to a deeply rooted tree with roots protruding from its trunk. It had an archaic look of both of wisdom and hardship. And as I sat upon its roots before me laid a small river and amongst the far bank were bushes and a tree with cotton like wisps falling with the breeze, carried by the air as if they were suspended in space as they fell to cover the river and surrounding nature with its seed. The river gleamed with the sun as the current moved everything in a path to the unknown. A snow drift of white cotton drifted in air before me as I stared deeply into nothing as I absorbed the nature that surrounded me. A carp along the bank searched for food a foot in front of me and I could see clearly its fins, head, and tail trusting as it was to live and search for sustenance. Deeply did I think of the past, present, and future both lonely from the thoughts of the past, restless from my present work bearing no fruit of sustenance but only of mind and heart did it fill but upsetting that it did not fill my belly or contribute financially for my family because as a man it only feels right to contribute and help those you love. The world is cruel I thought, both beautiful but bitter sweet. But I must give the sweet through the beauty of life none the less. Amongst the roots I sat with the snow drift cotton falling around me and thought only if life were always so serene and feelings of serenity fell around me for the rest of my life like the cotton within the air. Only if life was so simple as it is for the carp in the creek. But human was difficult for me. Never did I forget the time next to the tree that summer and visited the tree frequently to delve into thoughts of time and space, for time did not exist for me within nature's serenity only the space within my mind bound by my past but traversed through my passion to overcome all boundaries apparent to my understanding and a lack thereof about God, man, and the Universe. That time captured by my mind an imprint of thankfulness of a time on Earth amongst God in his nature and made me a better person by will of soul from the mind that never gave up understanding and a heart that beat compassion and trust in and for humanity. I hope all of life was so simple and serene but I guess all of nature thinks that way when they feel alone in their individuality amongst the nature that brings them closer to themself and to nature from nature returning them back to the nature that they are a part of in hopes to feel one with Earth that created them and have serenity enfold them in a loving embrace once more.

If the sun should rise with the waking trees as they stretch their limbs and open their leaves to the warmth and light it gives, will my heart open and my understanding stretch to the warmth and light that could not shine as bright from within me despite the brightness of faith and hope shining upon me so that I may touch all those who are open enough to care as I grow and live.

The hysteric laughter of a child is contagious. It is the best thing to catch in life other than the moment when they hold your finger.

Through it all I wonder if all was enough. If I had everything, if I knew everything, if everything was all that it is and will ever be would it give me happiness? I guess all happiness is was what I was thankful for and that was everything in itself which gave me thankfulness on the happiness I create in the future. It is easy to want everything when we are not thankful for what we have. Being thankful for what we have opens the door for everything to be in our life through wanting to be thankful toward having more. We just have to turn the knob by being thankful and never give up on opening doors to our future through wanting a better life.

Teaching should always be done as a means to teach the positive outcome to behaving rightfully so the person does not make the same mistakes. Even though we are often taught through feeling the repercussion to our actions it is necessary to prevent mistakes from occurring by giving more morale from positive actions not harmful ones. But only those who are forgiving but know how to wean know this.

What people didn't teach me was to embrace my humanity. I had to do that myself as I stepped out of other's judgments of how people should live and accept my humanity in its greatness both good and bad.

I guess perfection lays in embracing our own humanity so that we can embrace humanity so that we will be more of a moralizing factor than a demoralizing one so as we compete socially it is done in moderation as we seek a way to gain without harm to each other. And as we grow we will find that our potential is released at a constant frequency so that competing moderately is no longer a factor because what we give is good enough that others seek to compete with as we rise to our potential as we learn and give. Potential energy is always released as we find our abilities and through our abilities do we release our potential and ride it like a current to the expanse of the sphere of human involvement through the people we touch.

We all have ingenuity which is expressing our knowledge in a means to invent, be artistic, be witty, and express our understanding. Such ingenuity is a precursor for genius. However, genius is ingenuity expressed at a greater frequency as we find our potential through cultivating our abilities from knowing we have potential and finding a way to release it.

I only seek to be my best and seek not to survive but to live. I pray that one day I will earn the eternal life in heaven and be able to have a peaceful life but from now to nowhere I will give within the cycles of life God deems me worthy to live for him as I walk the stairway to heaven and I will walk it even if I have to build the staircase myself.

A woman is like a beautiful gift that is awaiting to be opened. And a woman knows this that is why she picks only one to receive her. Sometimes sharing with many who adore her for the gift within and the beauty that enfolds her. Enamored by both men and women alike.

A man is like marble but with a heart that melts to a woman's touch. A woman makes a man shine like the fire upon the curvatures of his form as she shines her beauty upon him and touches his heart from her love but strong with strength does a man's body and heart move with a force that is guided by his will. Willingness, will power, and a will to provide.
I don't know what to do. Left-right. Up-down. Good-bad. Right and wrong. I guess it all boils down to sink or float.

What I found is that life is to suffer at times. Sometimes at more times than others. It is a part of life. Forgive each other and our selves and let each others past lay as it is and what will grow is the good of the future. The soil has been turned and will not be re-turned, so we can settle for what will never be again or plant for the future in the present. Think not only of yourselves but for others before you return someone to their past through judgement or shame, for all has been planted for a reason. Forgive and move on for your self and others as we learn to be better as we approach living and not surviving.

What is inspiration other than a breath of fresh air that went unnoticed by some but empowered many through one. A one just like you.

Eternal life is grand but what is grand is the purpose we serve in life because eternal life is always there for us while our time on Earth is short. A piece of time that will never be the same again. I must make the best of it while I can.

If a light shines in darkness what gave the darkness a need for the light to exist? And if we are the lighthouses that steer the people away from harm then why did God put us in darkness to be the light that shines for others? Maybe that darkness is ignorance and the light is knowledge which is gained through perception to help others on their journey. Like ships with lanterns do we all let our light shine but some make it to port and be the light that guides many. I guess God made life difficult in order for us to exude our light to be the light for those who are in our lives so we may guide all those around us as we follow the brightest light of all, for it is the brightest light that clears the most darkness so that all may see the obstacles, the current flow of human involvement, and the dark entities that pull us off course so that we may stay on course through avoiding their trickery. But how do all lanterns shine brighter to be guiding lights for each other on our journey before we are the lighthouse that shines for many? By learning of self, life, logic, emotion, passion, and God as we seek to live a more virtuous life amongst our carnal nature and the ignorance that we all face because it is our bodies that cause us to make mistakes through our desires and intentions but also our lack of understanding. We must know the body and how it copes with life. We must understand emotion and how our perception effects our emotions as well as the ego and how it is effected by others so we may gain stability through preventing harm. We must know God in word but also in our self so we may live happier and we must care for our self more than we do for others so we may extend that care for our self to others, as we care for them as we do our self.

Rocks are stability, like Jesus was bringing to his people to have him be the rock in which people will learn of God as their faith in him from his care to heal that showed that he cared so that they will be open to receiving because as we all know people do not care unless they receive something to show that they are cared about until they learn to care unconditionally despite what they receive, so as Jesus healed did their faith in him have them be open to receive as they opened their hearts so that their minds will open to have the word touch their heart and recall the strength of faith in God within them and in doing so did God and Jesus become the rock in which they built upon through Jesus's faith which they found within themselves. Of course following Jesus do we make him our rock, one of many like fathers, mothers, mentors, and those of faith but as we know we all follow self because we are all individuals and as we follow Christ we do so as we understand his teachings and purpose in life so that through his teachings do we open our hearts to receive faith so we may understand God and humanity. But through it all do we find that as we follow Christ do we follow him through self to find our Christ self. Jesus said the stone that the builders reject I will make the capstone. He was making us strong in faith through being wiser people so we may be important for the structure of our community on which societies are built upon. Jesus's teachings were to enlighten so that we may follow self to gain stability through faith and community so we may follow self through understanding faith, humanity, and self to extend our fellowship through understanding. So, as we enlighten through our wisdom to guide those in our life and in the world do reach the rock within through our rock our lord but also God so that our light may shine from within upon a foundation of stability to guide others who seek a more stable life with understanding and faith so that the troubles in life can be overcame even from the aftermath of the troubles.

The biggest problem we have in life is making mistakes with each other. It is a learning experience to make us wiser so that we may shine our light brighter but the greatest thing to learn is to discern who is right for you and who is not, so those around you will shine together as you grow together. Some will depart, some will go on their own, some will move with others whose light shines different so that the light they exude will be through their desires and how they wish to seek understanding and stability. And as you make it to port and take the lighthouse upon the rock within from the understanding of self and the God within you may steer your people through your teachings and give your work, give your patience, responsibility, hope, and determination to be a good example as we grow into being better examples for them all. But remember this, to be human is to make mistakes and even though we eliminate the potential of making mistakes as we get older and wiser we still do make mistakes it is only natural. And to be the guiding light we must know this and learn from our mistakes but always give the good that we know so that we may be there in all ways from work to family despite our trivial mistakes. Life is to struggle with hardships but as we struggle together we find that we are not alone as we know that we are here for each other so why hold the mistakes of the past against someone whom has bettered themself when we have bettered our self despite our mistakes or hardship. To be the guiding light in its brilliancy and to be the one for many is in our hearts and is in our minds so that we may give plenty but a person's position does not only make one a guiding light but by the word from the heart and the love from the mind to give as we know we like to be given to through times of struggle and times of peace, for we are all people here for each other to be the light that shines in the mist of darkness. A darkness that is not so dark unless we make it that way for each other.

I guess when all is written I look back and to the future through reason to find purpose and why. I am a man. That's all I have been. . . a boy yes I have been also but I lived. I hope. . . I guess that was my strength. Faith. . . gave me purpose. Family. . . showed me love. God. . . was learned but also a discovery. . . I am blessed to have. Need. . . a value I found greater than want. Fear. . . because I love not only fear from survival but from loving did I fear losing but loved anyways with an open heart with no fear but with appreciation of love shared between souls their bodies, and people. Love. . . because it brings happiness for me and many. Knowledge. . . made me strong but what strength would that be for me when such knowledge is for the people? Been everything to everyone but nothing to me but a man and thankful was I to achieve the happiness I brought but hurt in knowing that sadness came from me to others as their sadness was from them to me in turn, I wish I could have prevented it all. A product of life none the less for sadness to happen. When all is said and done but written in word. . . I have given and hope what words of wisdom that I share may bring happiness, stability, understanding and a way for peace for a people and for the world. May this be a stone laid that will lay with the many works of those that will build the road to peace and a Way for the people to build through the wisdom and knowledge for the happiness and love for a people called humanity.

I thank you all but especially those who had faith in me and loved me unconditionally. As I write this I know not of my future, where I am headed, if I am to succeed or fail but what I do know is that I am a man who once lived and my thoughts, my passion, my soul, and words I give. I've done good and bad, rights and wrongs, and I a grow in spirituality as I get older to yet be spiritual enough. I hope you find happiness wherever you may be and find those who have faith in you and love you unconditionally. May time hold precious the expression of the mind, body, heart, and soul for all those who express themself. God bless and good bye.

Let us not only give food and shelter to the ones we love but let us give our time to build self esteem and encourage positive self expressions. Let us extend our virtue into our family so they may not only live a better life but treat others better as they move to better themselves while not accepting and overcoming wrong behavior. Let us extend from heart to hand our virtue through our family into society so others may learn of a better way of life to not only live and lead a better way of life but give a better way to those they love.

Sun's shadow falls,
the moon above aches,
time stops,
a moments whisper beneath the sky
recalls the symphony of men's lives.

- Joseph Roberts

The End